THE WORD FOR EVERY SEASON

Reflections on the Lectionary Readings

(CYCLE C)

Dianne Bergant, CSA

Paulist Press
New York/ Mahwah, NJ

also in this series by Dianne Bergant, CSA
The Word for Every Season (Cycle B)

Excerpts from the *Lectionary for Mass for Use in the Dioceses of the United States of America, second typical edition.* Copyright © 1970, 1997, 1998 Confraternity of Christian Doctrine, Inc., Washington, DC. All rights reserved. No part of this work may be reproduced or transmitted in any form or by any means, electronic or mechanical, including photocopying, recording, or by any information storage and retrieval system, without permission in writing from the copyright owner.

Scripture texts in this work are taken from the *New American Bible with Revised New Testament* © 1986, 1970, 1991 Confraternity of Christian Doctrine, Washington, DC, and are used by permission of the copyright holder. All rights reserved. No part of the *New American Bible* may be reproduced in any form without permission in writing from the copyright owner.

Most of these reflections originally appeared in "The Word" column of *America* magazine.

Cover photographs: Top left (maple tree) by Anton deFlon. Balance of photos courtesy of Shutterstock.

Cover design by Sharyn Banks
Book design by Lynn Else

Copyright © 2009 by the Congregation of St. Agnes

All rights reserved. No part of this book may be reproduced or transmitted in any form or by any means, electronic or mechanical, including photocopying, recording, or by any information storage and retrieval system without permission in writing from the Publisher.

Library of Congress Cataloging-in-Publication Data

Bergant, Dianne.
    The Word for every season : reflections on the lectionary readings (cycle C) / Dianne Bergant.
        p. cm.
    ISBN 978-0-8091-4607-9 (alk. paper)
    1. Church year meditations. 2. Bible—Meditations. 3. Catholic Church—Prayers and devotions. 4. Catholic Church. Lectionary for Mass (U.S.). Year C. I. Title.
    BX2170.C55B442 2009
    242'.3—dc22

                                                                2008054947

Published by Paulist Press
997 Macarthur Boulevard
Mahwah, New Jersey 07430

www.paulistpress.com

Printed and bound in the
United States of America

Contents

Introduction

The Catholic Bible Movement of the 1950s introduced us to what is known as the "historical-critical approach" to interpreting the Bible. This approach opened us to exciting new insights into the historical background of the stories with which we had become so familiar. What had often seemed baffling could now be better explained, and this without losing the religious mystery behind the biblical passage. Soon, even grade school children were devouring the fruits of this new method of interpretation.

Within the more recent past, we have gleaned new insights into biblical interpretation from various methods of literary criticism. This approach is not primarily interested in the concerns of the original author or the original biblical communities. It maintains that, once it leaves the original situation, the biblical text has a message in its own right, independent of the specific meaning of the author or the early communities.

This is similar to the case with music: One need not consult Bach to interpret one of his fugues. Everything needed for such an interpretation can be found in the score itself. So, everything needed for an interpretation of the Bible can be found within the Bible itself.

Over the years we have found that the employment of such interpretive approaches has enriched our understanding of the scriptures in ways too numerous to list. However, we maintain that the scriptures are more than religious texts meant to be studied with an eye to their importance to an ancient people, or as an example of well-crafted religious literature. We believe that the religious message that they contain is the foundation of our faith, and that somehow that religious message is meant to shape our own religious identity and to influence our behavior. We want to know what that message might mean for us today.

The reflections collected in this book are an attempt to address this final concern: What might that message mean for us today? These reflections spring from a careful examination of the lectionary readings for every Sunday and Solemnity of the liturgical year. Though at times historical or literary information might be offered, the focus here is on prayerful musing on the meaning that message might have for us today. It is in ways such as this that the word takes root in our hearts in and out of season.

Advent

FIRST SUNDAY OF ADVENT
Readings:
Jer 33:14–16; Ps 25:4–5, 8–9, 10, 14;
1 Thess 3:12—4:2; Luke 21:25–28, 34–36

READING THE "SIGNS OF THE TIMES"

One of the most exacting challenges posed by the Second
Vatican Council was the summons to read the "signs of the
times." It was a call to reflect deeply on the events unfolding
before our eyes and to respond to them out of mature faith. This
was a difficult task because many of us were accustomed to react-
ing to life rather than interacting with it, and few of us possessed
what today might be called "mature faith." We probably knew the
teachings of the church and were well grounded in genuine devotion, but we were passive rather than actively involved in critical
thinking about faith in its relation to our times.

This way of understanding our faith changed with the
Council. Over the years we have grown into a certain degree of
social sensitivity. We frequently take faith-based political stands.
At times we even turn a critical eye to the teachings and traditions
of the church, scrutinizing them and reinterpreting them when it
is deemed necessary. Our faith has matured and our devotion has
been enriched by reading the "signs of the times."

Today Jesus directs us: "When these signs begin to happen,
stand erect and raise your heads because your redemption is at
hand." Of which signs is he speaking? Is he really talking about
the end of the world? Should we all start reading cosmologists and
astrophysicists so that we know what to expect? Though such
reading would certainly enrich our appreciation of the universe of
which we are a part, Jesus is probably not talking about the cosmos. About what, then?

Jesus clearly tells us: "Your redemption is at hand." The days
that Jeremiah said were coming are now about to dawn, and we

3

are called to read the signs of their dawning. The prophet described these days as days of peace and fulfillment, of justice and security. This is certainly a very encouraging picture. The gospel paints a very different scene. It tells us that there will be suffering before these days really appear. And why will there be suffering? Because *we* have to be transformed, not the cosmos. Paul prays for our transformation. He prays that we will abound in love, that our hearts will be strengthened, that we will be blameless in holiness, that we will conduct ourselves to please God. The apocalyptic cosmic upheaval described is a powerful metaphor concerning the cost of such transformation, especially for those of us who are still rooted in anger and fear and deception, or in "carousing and drunkenness and the anxieties of daily life."

We know that the days of our redemption have already dawned with the coming of Jesus. Because our own transformation is always ongoing, however, we move yearly through the liturgical celebrations of the mystery of our salvation. Advent is set aside to commemorate Jesus' coming in the flesh as well as his final coming in glory, but it is also a time for us to open ourselves to the Lord's coming into our lives and our world today. In order to do this, we must read the "signs of the times."

One of the apocalyptic signs stated in the gospel is the dismay of nations. This is certainly evident today and, unlike many times in the past, we are all personally affected by it. Some of us know people who lost their lives in acts of terror or war. Fear has made us suspicious of people of other races or religious beliefs. Sometimes our anger has grown into revenge and our fear has taken on features of paranoia.

Some public officials have betrayed the trust we placed in them. They lied to us, misappropriated our money, and led us astray. Their own personal advantage seems too often to have been placed ahead of their responsibility to those of us who placed them in office. Our disapproval of their service has left many frustrated. Our inability to change the system has turned some away from any kind of civic involvement. The sinfulness of our church, a sinfulness we have always acknowledged as a fact of human frailty, has been revealed in all its heinousness. The beauty of the body of Christ has been marred by scandal, slander of the innocent, and disparagement of legitimate authority. Its shame is there for all to see.

If these are the signs of our times, how can we say that our redemption is at hand? Because these are not the only signs. In the face of all this dismay, we see heroism and patience and understanding; we see honesty and unselfish service of others; we see genuine holiness and fidelity. There are people in the world, in government, in the church, in our neighborhoods, and in our families who are committed to justice and peace. Their lives testify that the reign of God has indeed taken hold. Advent reminds us that we too can be transformed into that kingdom, and so this season calls to us all: "Stand erect and raise your heads because your redemption is at hand."

Praying with Scripture

- What positive "sign of the times" encourages you to transform your life?

- What negative "sign of the times" calls you to work for the transformation of the world?

- Make today's psalm a prayer for insight to recognize the "signs of the times" and for courage to respond appropriately.

SECOND SUNDAY OF ADVENT
Readings:
Bar 5:1–9; Ps 126:1–6;
Phil 1:4–6, 8–11; Luke 3:1–6

UNDER CONSTRUCTION!

In some parts of the country, it seems that there are only two seasons, winter and road construction. The excitement of a trip is often tempered by detours and long lines of single-lane traffic. Major sports events like the Super Bowl or the World Series, political conventions, or the upcoming visits of dignitaries also prompt the repair of our roads, though in such situations we usually discover routes that allow us to avoid any annoyance. Road repair is a fact of contemporary life.

Today's readings invite us to reflect on road construction. Baruch sketches a poignant scene. A devastated Jerusalem is instructed to put aside its grief, to clothe itself in splendor, and to stand on the heights in order to see its scattered children streaming back home from exile. Led away in shame by enemies, they are now brought back in glory by God. The road back home has been repaired for this great return. Impassable mountains have been brought low and ditches and gorges have been built up. Israel enjoys the advantages of the security that God's providence furnishes.

Luke alludes to a passage from Isaiah depicting a similar scene. In the original setting, the exiled people were told that God would lead them home, much like God had led their ancestors out of Egyptian bondage, through the wilderness, into the land of promise. The exiled people were assured that all obstacles would be removed from their path so this could be accomplished. In the gospel reading, Luke connects John the Baptist, who lived in the wilderness of Judea, with that voice "crying out in the desert." By implication, if John is the voice announcing the coming salvation by God, then Jesus is the one who will lead the people back home.

These readings do not focus on Jesus' coming *to* us, as some might expect Advent readings to do. Instead, they want us to think of his coming *with* us. He does not merely secure our salvation for us; he himself leads us to that salvation. It is because there are obstacles in our path that road construction or reform is necessary. This is not the kind of road repair that we can avoid by taking another route or by simply waiting until it is completed before we venture forth. We are involved in the reconstruction of this road, and we will have to move carefully on our way, repairing it as we travel over it.

What obstacles might we encounter that must be removed? As individuals, we might have to overcome deep-seated resentment, persistent faultfinding, unwillingness to forgive, dishonesty in our dealings with others, or a bullying attitude. We might be ruled by pride, or lust, or an insatiable desire to possess. There are obstacles in the life of every one of us that prevent us from hearing God's call or responding to it. Furthermore, the groups to which we belong also set up obstacles. There are some to which we may actively contribute; there are others from which we may simply benefit. As a society we might have to work to dismantle unfair housing policies, employment disparity, economic injustice, or racial and ethnic biases. We might have to be more active in opposing violence of any form, sexual exploitation of women and children, and the disregard for the integrity of creation. Renewal is a fact of life.

The image of a restored Jerusalem that was held out to the people of Israel encouraged them as they journeyed back home. The city they loved so dearly was now clothed in the "splendor of glory from God...wrapped in the cloak of justice." The image held out to us today is no less resplendent. It is the New Jerusalem, the new city of peace and justice, the reign of God on earth. The journey toward that city may be tedious, and the obstacles we encounter on the way may seem overwhelming, but God leads us just as God led the Israelites. The responsorial psalm reminds us that it was God who "brought back the captives of Zion." Just as "the LORD has done great things for them," so "the LORD has done great things for us." Our faith assures us of this, and we have Paul to spur us on. His words in today's reading are encouraging: "I am confident...that the one who began a good work in you will continue to complete it."

We may be puzzled by Advent readings that say nothing about Jesus' birth. What we are anticipating, however, is not simply the celebration of that single event, but the advent of our salvation. Its ultimate manifestation did indeed enter our world with Jesus' birth, but it takes root in our lives each time we respond to God's grace, and it will be brought to completion when Christ comes in glory. We are on the way to that ultimate destination. That is why we need a stretch of good road.

Praying with Scripture

- What in your personal life is an obstacle on the path to salvation? How might you remedy this?

- As you prepare for Advent, what one task might you perform to further the cause of justice and peace in the world?

- How might you function as John did, as one who prepares others for the coming of Jesus into their lives?

THIRD SUNDAY OF ADVENT
Readings:
Zeph 3:14–18a; Isa 12:2–6;
Phil 4:4–7; Luke 3:10–18

GOD IS IN OUR MIDST

We are at the midpoint of Advent, the Sunday known as *Gaudete*, the Sunday for rejoicing. It was so designated at a time when Advent was considered a penitential preparation for Christmas. Since penance is no longer the emphasis of this liturgical season, the Sunday seems to have lost some of its initial purpose. However, the rejoicing that it advocates continues to be in line with the season.

Advent is a time for joy, not primarily because we are anticipating the anniversary of the birth of Jesus, but because God is already in our midst. That is what the prophet Zephaniah claims, and in today's reading he makes that claim twice. He is speaking to a people who had been burdened with war and destruction and displacement. Their lives had been assaulted and their hopes dashed. In the face of this the prophet boldly directs them to "Shout for joy…sing joyfully….Be glad and exult." Given their circumstances, how could they possibly respond in this way?

The prophet assures them that with God in their midst, they can indeed move forward into a new life. In God's presence they have nothing further to fear. No longer do they stand under judgment, for they will be renewed in God's love. Are these empty promises? Can this really come to pass? It was up to Israel to decide whether they would turn to God and trust in the promises made to them, or continue on the path they had set for themselves.

Unfortunately, our world is not terribly different from theirs. It too is burdened with war and destruction and displacement; lives have been assaulted and hopes have been dashed. We are probably as skeptical about peace and restoration as were the ancient Israelites—perhaps even more so. But this skepticism need not prevent us from trusting that God will encircle us with love and will grant us the peace we so desperately seek.

Paul also calls us to rejoice. In fact, he says that we should rejoice always, because the Lord is near. There is no contradiction here regarding God's presence. Paul did not think that Christ was absent from our midst. Rather, he was speaking of Christ's final manifestation in glory. It is that time that is near; hence there is reason for rejoicing. But notice what else he says. In anticipation of that time of fulfillment, he admonishes us: "Your kindness should be known to all." Though peace and restoration are given to us by God, they do not simply drop down from heaven. We are involved in their fashioning. Still, we do not create this renewed world; God does. Furthermore, it is not given to us as a reward for our labors; it is fashioned within and through the very efforts of kindness that we make.

"What should we do?" This is the very question the crowds asked John the Baptist. We might expect this ascetic to make radical demands to leave everything and join him in the desert; adopt a life of fasting and penance. But John does not make such demands. Instead, he calls people to fidelity in the very circumstances of their own lives: Those who have more than they need should share with those who have less; tax collectors are to be honest; soldiers are not to take advantage of the vulnerable; parents are to cherish their children; spouses are to be faithful; neighbors are to live in peace.

John models an attitude of mind and heart that is needed in today's world. Though he was eccentric, he was very popular. People from every walk of life thronged to him. While some no doubt came out of curiosity, others were clearly motivated by religious fervor. They sought his advice about the direction their lives should take. John could have taken great pride in his reputation and in the influence that this probably afforded him, but he did not. Quite the contrary! He knew who he was, and he knew who he was not. He did not use his influence to enhance his prestige. He was an honest man, a man of humility.

We cannot fail to wonder how much of the world's sorry state is not the consequence of arrogance, arrogance stemming from military prowess, or economic prosperity, or educational superiority. People and nations less fortunate are sometimes minimized or treated as inferiors. Resentment turns to hatred, and hatred breeds violence. But this does not have to be the case. It is precisely this world filled with resentment and hatred and violence that can be transformed. It is precisely in and through our efforts to rid this world of such a scourge that the new world is fashioned, the reign of God is brought forth.

Are these empty promises? Can this really come to pass? It is now up to us to decide whether we will turn to God and trust in the promises made to us, or continue on the path we have set for ourselves. God is in our midst! Rejoice!

Praying with Scripture

- How is God's presence among us made known to you?

- Do you really believe that God can establish peace and restoration in our world? If not, why not?

- To what particular behavior is John the Baptist's admonition calling you?

FOURTH SUNDAY OF ADVENT
Readings:
Mic 5:1–4a; Ps 80:2–3, 15–16, 18–19;
Heb 10:5–10; Luke 1:39–45

STANDING ON THE THRESHOLD

Something that can only be described as electric is felt in a crowd waiting in a line, anxious for doors to be opened. This is true at a movie or a sports event, on the first day of a sale, or the first day of school. The anticipation is almost palpable. People can hardly wait; they feel that they are on the threshold of something marvelous. That is where we find ourselves. The readings prepare us for the upcoming feast, giving us glimpses into the mysteries that we will be celebrating. They bring together the major themes of the first three Sundays of Advent, namely, promise, repentance, transformation, and joy. We now stand on the threshold, eager for the doors to be opened so that we can step inside and enjoy the marvels prepared for us there.

Today's readings open the door a crack, and we are amazed that everything inside seems so ordinary. We see Bethlehem, an unsophisticated little village that is but a stone's throw from the thriving capital, Jerusalem. It is so unassuming that today we might miss it on the road were there not a sign marking its borders. Though it was remembered by the people of Jesus' time as the birth-place of the great king David, it really never made a name for itself in any other way. If we look further through the crack in the door, to the side we will see a young pregnant woman hastening to help an older relative who is also with child. There is nothing extraordi-nary about this either, especially in a society that is so family ori-ented. Young women acted in this way. Catching these glimpses of ordinary life we might ask: Just what is God up to?

The reading from the prophet Micah tells us that a ruler even greater than King David will come from this rugged backwater village. A shepherd will be born there unlike any shepherd who routinely tended flocks in the hills that surround the simple dwellings of that village. The gospel writer tells us that something extraordinary occurred between the two women depicted in the gospel story. The lives that were growing within the sanctuaries of their wombs recognized each other. This astonishing encounter took place out in the open, yet no one saw it. Once again we might ask: Just what is God up to?

Why does God choose what is ordinary to carry the radiance of the divine? Might it be so that the glory is not given to the com-mon, ordinary vessel that holds that radiance, but redounds to God to whom it really belongs? Furthermore, is it possible that we overlook the unpretentious through which God is revealed and mistake what is loud and flashy for what is truly marvelous?

Whatever the case may be, God's choices recounted in today's readings should encourage all of us. They insist that the mystery of the incarnation comes to ordinary people living ordinary lives. All that is required is an openness to do God's will, a willingness to respond to God's call.

According to the author of the Letter to the Hebrews, such obedience was the motivating force in Jesus' life. Contrary to what many have thought, God is not interested in our sacrifices, holocausts, and sin offerings. Rather, God desires an open and willing heart: "Behold, I come to do your will, O God." It was with such a heart that Mary accepted God's plan for her, thus making her "Blessed…among women." It was with such a heart that Elizabeth welcomed Mary into her home, and in this act welcomed the long-awaited Messiah as well. And what kind of heart do we carry as we await the fulfillment of God's promises?

As we stand on the threshold of the feast of the Incarnation, we begin to realize that the events of God's loving plan of salvation do not need a flamboyant stage on which to unfold. They can take place on a farm in the heartland of the country, on a quiet street of a small town, in a simple apartment of a bustling city. The radiance of God can shine forth through the faithfulness in the ordinary events of life—a shepherd tending sheep, a mechanic repairing a car, a young woman attentive to the needs of another, an expectant mother preparing for her firstborn child. What appear at first glance to be ordinary places, common people, and everyday events are the channels through which the grace of God comes to us.

Something exciting is about to happen, something truly electrifying! Divine love is about to break through the commonplace and shine forth in our world. We stand on the threshold of this wondrous event, but are we ready? Will our minds and hearts be open so that we can recognize it when it appears? We pray with today's responsorial psalm: "Lord, make us turn to you; let us see your face and we shall be saved" (Ps 80:4).

Praying with Scripture

- Might you be overlooking certain persons in your life because you do not believe that they are important enough?

- In what small situations do you already see the glory of God?

- Pray for the grace to recognize the extraordinary in what may seem only ordinary.

Christmas
Season

CHRISTMAS (C)
Readings:
(Midnight) Isa 9:1–6; Ps 96:1–3, 11–13;
Titus 2:11–14; Luke 2:1–14; (Dawn) Isa 62:11–12;
Ps 97:1, 6,11–12; Titus 3:4–7; Luke 2:15–20;
(Day) Isa 52:7–10; Ps 98:1–6;
Heb 1:1–6; John 1:1–18

OUR SAVIOR, CHRIST THE LORD

The feast of Christmas is so rich in religious themes that we need three sets of readings to throw light on its meaning, and even then we only scratch the surface. At midnight we are struck by the contrast between a child wrapped in swaddling clothes, as we find in the gospel account, and the Father-Forever of whom Isaiah speaks. This child who is the Prince of Peace is born into a people living under the heel of Roman occupation. The Wonder-Counselor lies in a manger and is surrounded by ordinary farm animals. The glorious news of the birth of the God-Hero is announced to simple shepherds, not the kind of people to whom those in authority would listen. The contrast found in these readings underscores some of the paradoxes of the Christian faith, paradoxes that are in the forefront of the mystery of the incarnation.

Down through the centuries, these contrasts have inspired numerous Christmas cards. The royal titles found in the prophecy of Isaiah accompany scenes of a child in a manger or shepherds on a hillside. It may be that we are so familiar with these depictions that we take the paradoxes lightly. When we receive such Christmas cards, do we ever spend time contemplating the scenes of the glorious event we are celebrating together, or is the name on the card our primary interest? Has the message of Christmas art inspired us? Are we astounded by God's graciousness shown to us? Have we come to realize how much God loves those who are weak and vulnerable and away from the limelight? Have we forgotten that we too are weak and vulnerable and probably on the sidelines? Or are we too busy with the tasks to be accomplished, gatherings to be enjoyed, and gifts to be exchanged—all important endeavors but not primary concerns?

Midnight Mass is a time of deep silence, a time for prayerful reflection. It is a time for us to pause and consider the manner in which God chose to save us. The reading from the Letter to Titus reminds us that Christmas is more than a time of nostalgia and warm feelings. The birth of this child announces that "the grace of God has appeared, saving all." This feast and the grace that it promises call us "to live temperately, justly, and devoutly in this age."

A sense of wonder appears in the readings for the Mass at dawn. The people in the days of Isaiah needed to be assured that their salvation had dawned. The reading suggests a degree of hesitancy, like the light of day shyly creeping up over the horizon. At first its light is subdued, but then it shines forth in all its brilliance. The shepherds depicted in the gospel reading are also amazed. But why? This was certainly not the first newborn they had ever seen. Nor would they have been surprised by the surroundings in which they found the child. They themselves might have spent nights in similar shelters. But this child's birth had been announced to them by angels. And if the heavenly announcement was accurate—"an infant wrapped in swaddling clothes"—then perhaps the rest of it was true as well: "a savior has been born."

This scene has also been captured in Christmas cards. It too challenges us. We take children to the crib so that they can wonder at the birth of the baby Jesus. Have we been able to hold on to the wonder that we see in the eyes of children? Or have we failed to grasp the depth of faith that prompted the shepherds to leave what was familiar and venture into the unknown? Has the harshness of life squelched our passion for living with excitement? Do we see each sunrise as a promise of new life? The reading from the Letter to Titus assigned to this Mass reminds us that "the kindness and generous love of God our savior appeared, not because of any righteous deeds we had done but because of his mercy." We should remember this as we stand before the crib.

The readings for the third Mass on Christmas are for grown-ups. There are no Christmas cards here. Instead, we are invited to look deeply into the identity of this child who is more than a child. He is the Word of God, the very self-expression of God. He was present at creation; he was actually the one through whom all things were made. This description is not a departure from the picture of the helpless child in the manger. In fact, traces of this marvel can be seen in the very first reading for midnight Mass: "Wonder-Counselor, God-Hero, Father-Forever, Prince of Peace." A comparable characterization of this child is found in the reading from the Letter to the Hebrews. He is the refulgence of God's glory, the very imprint of God's being. The Christmas readings begin and end with this theological portrayal. It serves as a frame around the Bethlehem picture, keeping us mindful of who this child really is and why he was born—our Savior, Christ the Lord!

Praying with Scripture

- How might the simplicity of the Christmas scene be calling you to simplify your own life?

- In what ways might you give more of yourselves to the people in your life?

- Make a point to pray the Christmas psalms during this week.

HOLY FAMILY
Readings:
Sir 3:2–7, 12–14; Ps 128:1–5; Col 3:12–21; Luke 2:41–52

HONOR LIFE—IN ITS EARLY YEARS AND IN ITS DECLINE!

"Honor thy father and thy mother." We all know this injunction as the fourth commandment. We learned it as children, along with the other nine commandments. In our very earliest years, that might have been the only commandment for us, since if we obeyed our parents we would be going to church and respecting the property of others. We would not fight or steal, and we certainly would not be using "bad language." Since our young lives were in a way circumscribed by that commandment, we might think that it was originally intended for children; at least, that is the way it was probably presented to us. Actually, it *was* intended for children, but more for adult children than for younger ones. Most likely, we learned later in life that the commandments were part of God's covenant pact made with the Israelites, a pact requiring adult participation. So we can presume from this that all the commandments without exception were directed toward adults.

The first reading from Sirach confirms this when it insists that respect extends to a parent even when that parent is suffering some form of diminishment, perhaps particularly at such a time. This passage expresses what can only be described as true "family values." It insists that respect is due both the father and the mother, an interesting prescription from a society grounded in patriarchal values. The author of Sirach may not have valued women generally (Sir 9:2–9; 42:14), but he certainly ordered respect for mothers. Finally, it is clear that the author also values children, for a new generation of children is promised as the blessing for those who respect their parents.

Many modern societies seem to lack the kind of respect for elders noted in this reading, though it is found in more traditional societies today. Not only is this a shame, but it is also our loss. Our history is inscribed in the memories of the elders; the wisdom that we need for successful living is imprinted on their hearts. They have watched fads come and go, and they know from experience what in life has lasting value. If we really respected our parents and all of the elder members of society, we would always honor them. We would give them the financial assistance they need so that they would never have to choose between required medication and nourishing food. We would see to it that the elderly shut-ins would not have to suffer devastating loneliness along with the burden of age and diminishment.

The child Jesus knew that his elders were the repositories of wisdom and tradition. That is why, as today's gospel reading recounts, he stayed in the Temple listening to the teachers and asking them questions while his family set out for home after celebrating the feast of Passover in Jerusalem. Then, even though he identified God as his Father, he went back to Nazareth with his parents, where he was obedient to them.

Another group that modern society sometimes neglects is the children. We love our babies. They are so cute, so adorable! But we often overlook our youngsters whose clothes might be wrinkled or ripped or dirty, and who are missing a tooth or two. When the "awkward age" sets in, we frequently forget how cute they once were and how good looking they will probably grow to be. At that stage, they simply annoy us with their rowdiness and rebellion, and sometimes with their incessant questioning. We claim that we want a good education for the children, but we do not always provide the funds that will give them access to the most qualified instructors. We do not always insist that the children be steeped in the traditions of our faith and in the history, literature, and art of civilization. When we fail to do this, we rob them of their heritage.

If we really loved our children, not merely those who are our own flesh and blood but all of the children of our society, we would not tolerate any form of child abuse. We would vigorously oppose child trafficking or child pornography everywhere in the world. We would insist that their teachers will be competent and dedicated; that all school buildings be safe from violence and in good repair; that the curricula prepare them for their future and instill in them appreciation for the things in life that are good and beautiful. If we really loved our children, we would teach them to love others and to commit themselves to fashioning a better world.

It is so easy to become impatient with both our elderly and our children. So often they do not conform to what we insist is best for them. We sometimes resist their independence and penalize them for exerting it. It is all so much easier when they obey. This is not always the best policy, however. Paul instructs us today in how we are to live in our families. He exhorts us to be filled with "heartfelt compassion, kindness, humility, gentleness, and patience." Such sentiments cross generational lines. They flow from the kind of love that creates and strengthens family ties. They are the kind of sentiments that can make our families truly holy families.

Praying with Scripture

- Make an effort this week to show concern and respect to an elderly person.

- Let at least one child know that you have that child's best interest in mind.

- Reach out to a member of your own family with whom you might not have had contact for some time.

SOLEMNITY OF THE BLESSED VIRGIN MARY
Readings:
Num 6:22–27; Ps 67:2–3, 5–6, 8; Gal 4:4–7; Luke 2:16–21

"WHAT CHILD IS THIS?"

Did Mary understand how amazing her child was? Does any mother? We love our children and celebrate every little thing about them, but no one really knows the potential hidden deep within that squirming bundle of humanity. True, whenever a child is born, there are always those who gather around and marvel at how perfectly every finger has been formed, and even how healthy the lungs sound. But the amazement that surrounded *this* child was significantly different from what normally occurs. His conception was announced by an angel, and other heavenly beings heralded his birth. Perfect strangers came to marvel at him, and Magi from the East came to pay homage. Mary had a right to wonder: "What child is this?"

It is quite clear, from all of the Christian stories, that Mary had much to ponder, and ponder she did. In this she is a model for all of us. She inspires us to consider deeply the significance of the events of which we are a part. These events may not include the kind of wondrous circumstances that attended her life, but we cannot deny that they challenge us to look beneath the surface in order to discover their real meaning. For example: As we as a society insist on protecting unborn life, we must also do everything we can to nourish that life after it sees the light of day. Our interest and attention should not end with the helpless infant, but should also extend to the young family that might be in need. As we move through this Christmas season of joy, we cannot afford to turn a blind eye to the reality of the world within which we find ourselves, a world of terror and fear and war, a world not so different from the one into which Jesus was born.

Mary's head was not turned by the marvelous things that had come to pass. She did not exempt herself or her son from their religious obligations. Rather, she, along with Joseph, saw to it that he was circumcised on the eighth day as the law prescribed. Following her example, we too must seek to do God's will for us today. True, the Second Vatican Council lifted many of the requirements that formerly defined the religious lives of many of us. As a result, we may not be sure about what really defines us today as Catholics. It may very well be that we must now ponder this question more than we did in the past. It may be that discovering God's will for us is more difficult than following it once it is discovered. But even in this, Mary stands out as an example. It was probably not difficult having the boy circumcised, but how was she supposed to raise him, a child whose very being seemed to radiate God? How could she bring him back to Nazareth and act as if nothing unusual had happened? Mary had much to ponder, and ponder she did.

The short passage from Paul's Letter to the Galatians simply mentions Mary as the one through whom Jesus was born into the world. However, it is rich in trinitarian theology. It states that Jesus, the son of Mary, was also the Son of God, and it was as Son of God that he made it possible for us all to be daughters and sons of God. How is this possible? "God sent the Spirit of his Son into our hearts, crying out, 'Abba, Father!'" Here we see the Father, the Son, and the Spirit. How does Mary fit into this? If we are made children of God through the Son of God, would not that same Son who was also the son of Mary make us children of Mary?

The first day of the New Year is traditionally celebrated as a day to pray for peace. Following Mary's example, we must ponder deeply the events in our world, in our country, in our church, and in our families that cry out for genuine and lasting peace. Why is it that we do not seem to be able to achieve peace? Might it be that we really do not grasp its true meaning? The Hebrew word *shalom* really means "completeness, wholeness, harmony, fulfillment." Such peace can only be achieved if everyone, not just some, has what she or he needs to live with dignity and integrity. True peace will not be attained through a show of force. As Pope Paul VI said: "If you want peace, work for justice."

So many Christmas cards wished us peace, but did they also provide any suggestions as to how we might attain it? The prayer of Aaron, found in today's first reading, given to the Israelites when they were in the wilderness, is offered to us today. "The LORD look upon you kindly and give you peace!" It acknowledges that peace is a blessing from God, not the reward of a show of might. There could not be a better New Year greeting.

Praying with Scripture

- Following the example of Mary, spend some time today pondering the goodness of God in your life.

- Pray the responsorial psalm slowly, asking for the insight to recognize God's will for you.

- What can you do to foster peace in the world, in the church, or in your family?

SECOND SUNDAY AFTER CHRISTMAS
Readings:
Sir 24:1–2, 8–12; Ps 147:12–15, 19–20;
Eph 1:3–6, 15–18; John 1:1–5, 9–14

HE PITCHED HIS TENT AMONG US

Most of the readings of the Christmas season carry us back hundreds of years to the city of Jerusalem or to the "little town of

Bethlehem." There we see the unassuming couple with the new-born child, the simple and probably foul-smelling shepherds, and the mysterious travelers from the East bringing gifts that might qualify as a king's ransom. The scenes depicted in today's readings are otherworldly. They lift us out of the terrestrial world that we know so well into the cosmic realms, and there we get a glimpse of another side of this helpless infant. Here he is neither helpless nor an infant.

In the first reading we find Woman Wisdom explaining the circumstances of her settlement in the land of Israel. She could have taken up residence anywhere in the world. I might have presumed that the logical choice would have been Athens with its highly reputed, sophisticated culture. According to the reading, however, God decided that Wisdom would dwell in Jerusalem, thus demonstrating the superiority of the religious tradition of Israel over the awe-inspiring philosophy of the Greeks. Following God's directions, Wisdom then pitched her tent in the chosen city, Jerusalem.

This tradition undoubtedly influenced the author of the Gospel of John in which we find Jesus characterized as the Word or *Logos* (Greek) of God. Like Wisdom before him (Sir 24:3–6), this Word enjoyed an intimate relationship with the Creator; like Wisdom before him, he was present at creation itself; like Wisdom before him, he far surpasses anything that a mere human being might achieve. Wisdom's teachings shine forth like light (Sir 24:30), while the Word is the light itself that shines forth in the darkness. On the other hand, there are significant differences between the two. For example, Wisdom is accepted by her people; "she is exalted…she is admired…she finds praise…she is blessed." The Word, on the other hand, "came to what was his own, but his own people did not accept him." It should be noted that both Wisdom and the Word are glorified in the cosmic realm. It is among the people of earth that their reception differs. Wisdom is desired by all; while the Word, like the infant who was a threat to the royal household of Jerusalem, is rejected by some.

The benediction with which the passage from the Letter to the Ephesians opens is also cosmic in nature. The image is that of God reigning from the heavens, entrusting our Lord Jesus Christ with the power to grant us blessings. The author goes on to say that not only was Christ present before the foundation of the world, but we too were chosen in him at that time, chosen "to be holy and without blemish before him." Christ is the Son of God, bringing to fulfillment all the glory and privilege associated with the figure of Woman Wisdom. Through Christ we enjoy the privileges that accompany our status as adopted children of God. The Christmas message proclaimed by the angels promised salvation to the entire world. This passage claims that our salvation was not merely an afterthought as a result of human sin, but was in God's plan from the very beginning. It also makes clear the divine reason for this gift of salvation: "In love he destined us…in accord with the favor of his will, for the praise of the glory of his grace."

The message of the readings for this Sunday corresponds with that of the third Mass for Christmas. In fact, the same gospel passage is read at both liturgies. Lest the very human sentiments of simplicity and childlike devotion cloud our vision of the profound meaning of the incarnation, we are reminded again of the magnitude of divine condescension. The Word of God, through whom all things were made, deigned to become one of us. Taking human flesh, he pitched his tent among us. We will never be able to grasp the meaning of this demonstration of God's immeasurable love for us. One would think that our response to it would be overwhelming gratitude and praise. As inconceivable as it may seem, however, we often meet this divine generosity with rejection.

The true light has come into our world, and we sometimes prefer the darkness. We would rather be swallowed up by consumerist habits that often undermine our health or clutter our lives than live simply so that others can simply live. We would rather insist on national pride that borders on stubborn arrogance than take steps to negotiate conflicts with the attitude of respect for our differences. We would rather hold grudges for years, perhaps even a lifetime, than forgive as we have been forgiven.

There are those, however, who do believe in his name. It is up to us to number ourselves among them. As adopted children of God, we have been called to live in the light. It is up to us to accept the invitation.

Praying with Scripture

- Society often chooses the wisdom of the world over that of any religious tradition. Pray for the grace to overcome the temptation to act in this way.

- Spend some time reflecting on the magnitude of divine generosity in your life.

- In what ways does your life radiate the true light brought into this world by Jesus Christ?

EPIPHANY
Readings:
Isa 60:1–6; Ps 72:1–2, 7–8, 10–13;
Eph 3:2–3a, 5–6; Matt 2:1–12

YOU LIGHT UP MY LIFE!

We have just passed the winter solstice, the shortest day of the year. We will now enjoy a little more light each day. Christmas itself is a feast of lights. Trees are brought into homes and made radiant with brilliant lights; yards and streets are also illumined; stores are decorated with lights. The whole world seems to be illuminated. In other ways too, our lives are aglow with light. Families come together and are sometimes reunited after many years; bonds of love and friendship are strengthened by kind wishes and gift-giving, and memories are brought back to life while new memories are given birth. These events of grace truly light up our lives.

The readings for today speak of two kinds of light. Isaiah promises a light full of hope. Years earlier the city of Jerusalem and the entire nation of Israel had gone through defeat at the hands of the Babylonians. The city was destroyed, and the land was devastated. The people were either killed, left to die of their wounds or of starvation, or forced into exile in the land of their conquerors. After more than an entire generation of captivity in

Babylon, they were now about to return to their own land and rebuild their lives. Forced migration is a painful reality that has been repeated down through the ages, even to our own day. And yet the prophet proclaims that the darkness of despair has been lifted, and a new day of restoration has dawned. At last, the light has come!

A different light is described in the gospel passage. There we read that the Magi were led to the child by the light of a star. Several explanations of this remarkable heavenly sight have been given. Some interpreters suggest that it was a supernova or a comet; others believe that it resulted from the alignment of two or more planets. Those who interpret all the details of the Christmas stories literally maintain that the star was a unique astrological occurrence, never seen before or since. Finally, others consider the star a literary element of the story, one that carries profound religious meaning. Whether this star was an actual celestial phenomenon or a metaphor for some other kind of enlightenment, all interpreters agree that it was a sign of an extraordinary event as well as a form of divine guidance that led the Magi to the child.

The children's version of the gospel story is well known to most. Who has not sung or heard the Christmas carol "We Three Kings," or who has not stood in awe of the magnificent gifts that these men presented to the child? Gold is a treasure that everyone might covet; frankincense and myrrh captivate the imagination because of their exotic nature. All of this adds to the astounding character of the birth of this child. It is the adult version of the story, however, that contains the real challenge. It maintains that God is the source of our life, not the social, political, or even religious structures of the day. It teaches that openness, humility, and the willingness to risk are necessary if we, like the Magi, hope to read correctly the signs of the times and to follow faithfully what we might learn from them. It insists that when we discover the "promised one," we must be willing to offer him all that we have.

Besides focusing on various aspects of light, all of today's readings touch on the theme of universalism. The gospel passage does not identify the land of origin of the Magi, but it does indicate that they came from the East and that they eventually returned to their own country. They did homage to the child, but there is no mention of them relinquishing their own religious allegiance. The angel announced that the child would be the savior of the entire world; these men were the firstfruits of that universal promise. The first reading declares that the treasures from the foreign lands of Midian, Ephah, and Sheba will be brought to the restored city of Jerusalem. The international scope of the influence of the Israelite king is proclaimed in the responsorial psalm. Tarshish, the Isles, Arabia, and Seba will pay him tribute. Finally, the Letter to the Ephesians declares that the Gentiles will be "coheirs, members of the same body, and copartners in the promise in Christ Jesus through the gospel."

God's graciousness to nations other than Israel challenges us today, enmeshed as we are in religious conflict. This conflict can range from religious condemnation of those who understand the Christian message differently from the way we do, to armed battle against a nation considered the "evil empire" or the "great Satan." The readings for today depict the "other" person as acceptable to God even when that "other" does not change religious loyalties. The light promised today should enable us to recognize this. The light has come, and we have been invited to live in it. How have we responded to that invitation?

Praying with Scripture

- Make a point to learn something about a religious tradition other than your own.

- Pray for the openness to follow wherever God leads you.

- What in today's gospel passage made the most impression on you? How might you respond to it?

BAPTISM OF THE LORD (C)
Readings:
Isa 42:1–4, 6–7; Ps 29:1–4, 9–10;
Acts 10:34–38; Luke 3:15–16, 21–22

THROUGH THE WATERS TO NEW LIFE

The Christmas season closes with the feast of the Baptism of the Lord. This marks not merely the end of things, but rather a new beginning. The readings remind us that the one born of our flesh is the servant of God, the very Son of God who brings a promise of justice and hope to a world in desperate need. They focus our attention on various aspects of this mystery. In a certain sense, they are like a montage of snapshots, each one providing a glimpse of Jesus' true identity. They fill us with awe, and also with the desire to join our own fate with this extraordinary person.

The passage from the prophet Isaiah is the first of four sketches of the mysterious "servant of the LORD" found in that biblical book. Endowed with God's own spirit, this figure is the agent of God's saving power. He brings justice to the nations, not through force of might but with tenderness and solicitude for the weak and vulnerable. He is "light for the nations," teaching them, opening their eyes, leading them out of prison. He is identified by God as "my servant...with whom I am pleased, upon whom I put my spirit."

The gospel writer recounts the event of Jesus' baptism by John. The Baptist acknowledges that, though his baptism with water is important as a sign of repentance, the baptism of the one coming after him will be much more significant. With the Holy Spirit and with fire, he will purge and transform. Then, in order to show that Jesus fulfills the expectations associated with the Isaian "servant of the LORD," John reports that when "heaven was opened and the Holy Spirit descended upon [Jesus]" he was identified with the words: "You are my beloved Son; with you I am well pleased." Jesus is the agent of God's saving power par excellence. He will bring justice to the nations, not through force of might but with tenderness and solicitude for the weak and vulnerable. He will be the true "light for the nations," teaching them, opening their eyes, leading them out of prison.

The story of the conversion of the household of the Roman centurion Cornelius illustrates the effect of this light in the lives of the Gentiles. Peter's words at that time are telling: "In truth, I see that God shows no partiality. Rather, in every nation whoever fears him and acts uprightly is acceptable to him." The universality of the good news of the gospel, a major theme of the feast of the Epiphany, is found today as well.

Though the readings for this Sunday would have us concentrate on the person and ministry of Jesus, they contain a challenge for us as well. According to Isaiah, the ministry of the servant is one of justice for all and tenderness toward those who have been broken. According to the Gospel of Luke, the ministry of Jesus will be one of purification and transformation. According to the passage from Acts of the Apostles, the disciples of Jesus widen the scope of that ministry to include the Gentile world. That same ministry, with the same divine approval, has now been given to us. Our own baptism brought us into the circle of the children of God and commissioned us to continue the work begun by Jesus. And what might this entail?

We live in a time of great unrest. The world seems poised on the brink of chaos; businesses and individuals face financial instability; the turmoil within the church threatens its longstanding foundation. No one is untouched by some form of the chaos that threatens to swallow us up alive. Where can we turn when the institutions meant to be our refuge from chaos are themselves the source of its threat? In the Bible, chaos is frequently portrayed as unruly water threatening to wipe out every living thing (e.g., the flood in Genesis). Today's responsorial psalm reminds us in no uncertain terms: "The LORD is enthroned above the flood." It assures us that God rules over the chaos in which we find ourselves. The response invites us to trust in God; Isaiah offers us a plan for restoring order; Acts challenges us to continue the work of Jesus. As he came forth from the waters of the Jordan, Jesus' life took a new direction. As his followers, we emerged from the waters of baptism as new people who, with God's help, are capable of countering the chaos of our world with justice and tender care of others.

On this day we do not look back to Christmas with nostalgia, sorry that the excitement and joy of the season has now come to a close. Rather, we look forward to the task ahead of us, the task that we have inherited from Jesus himself, realizing that at our baptism God proclaimed: "Here is my servant whom I uphold."

Praying with Scripture

- How in your life do you foster justice and care for the weak and vulnerable?

- In what ways might your life proclaim the good news to those who do not share your faith tradition?

- Using your own words, renew your baptismal promises to avoid the temptations of the word and to live as a child of God.

Lent

FIRST SUNDAY OF LENT
Readings:
Deut 26:4–10; Ps. 91:1–2, 10–15;
Rom 10:8–13; Luke 4:1–13

SALVATION IS A GIFT!

Strange as it may seem, it is very difficult for many of us to accept gifts. When we do receive them, we feel compelled to reciprocate in kind. We often believe that we must earn what we get. Perhaps we do not want to be beholden to others, or we are convinced that we do not deserve any such gift. Or maybe we want to be assured that what is ours is really ours, with no strings attached.

In a slightly different vein, we are also convinced that we must make up time lost at school or at work. There is a certain level of performance that is expected by us and by others, and we are bound to meet it and, if possible, to exceed it. Too often we gauge our worth by the quality of our accomplishments.

These attitudes often carry over into our understanding of our faith, particularly during Lent. We perceive this season as a time to make amends, to perform acts of devotion or self-discipline that will balance the scales. This is quite futile, because we will really never be able to balance the scales. If we look carefully at the readings for Lent, we will discover that God does not require this of us. The readings for the entire season show us that salvation is a gift from God, not a reward earned.

All of the first readings for the Sundays of Lent recount episodes from Israel's history that show God's graciousness to the people. The passages from the epistles all highlight the role that Christ played in our salvation. The gospel readings reveal Jesus' glory even in the face of suffering, as well as the compassion and mercy of God. Any call to repentance is only indirect. The readings assure us how much God has loved us. They insist that we should be grateful, trust in God, and, if necessary, reform our lives.

Today's reading from Deuteronomy is one of the most important creedal statements in the Old Testament. It describes God's initial call to Abraham and God's graciousness in delivering the Israelite people. The people turned to God in their need, and God saved them from bondage in Egypt. The sacrifice that they offered was one, not of reparation, but of thanksgiving for God's goodness. The psalm response also proclaims God's protection and assistance of those in need. There is no quid pro quo here, no "if you do this, I'll do that." God's goodness is pure gift.

Paul insists on the same point. He argues that it is not good works that save us, but faith or openness to God. He must have startled his audience when he declared that membership in the Jewish community gave one no advantage. This should startle us as well. It is not membership in the correct religious group, but genuine faith that justifies us.

The gospel recounts the temptations of Jesus. Many commentators maintain that these represent some of the prominent messianic expectations of his day. The people believed that the Messiah would feed the hungry, or release the nation from the domination of others, or call on the extraordinary power of God to perform miracles. These were all admirable deeds in themselves; they still are today. Who would not want to see that the hungry are well fed, or that people are granted self-determination? Who would not want to demonstrate the marvelous power of God? Then why are these good works presented here as temptations? Might it be that Jesus is challenged to perform them for the wrong reasons? It seems that real temptation is often subtle, not obvious, and we too are frequently tempted to do good things, but for the wrong reasons or in inappropriate ways.

In the face of each temptation, Jesus reminds the tempter that the heart of righteousness is commitment to God, not the performance of marvelous deeds. Jesus will indeed eventually feed the hungry, deliver the people from bondage, and demonstrate the marvelous power of God. But he will accomplish these feats in God's good time and in a manner that will please God and not the crowds. Jesus never bargained for results.

What do these readings tell us about Lent? They show no interest in what we can do for God, but in what God has done for us. They call us, not primarily to repent of our sins, but rather to open our hearts to God in faith. Even the account of Jesus' temptations underplays the significance of great feats of devotion, but instead emphasizes the importance of fidelity to God's promptings in life.

This is not to say that penance is out of place during Lent. Quite the contrary. Still, whatever we take on should enable us to recommit ourselves to God who has been so gracious to us. It should strengthen our faith and trust in God, and not reassure us that we have paid our debts. It should open our eyes to the fact that God is indeed our refuge and our fortress, the source of our salvation, the one in whom we can trust.

Praying with Scripture

- Recall the many ways in which God has stepped into your life as savior, and give thanks for God's goodness.

- In what subtle ways might you be susceptible to temptation? How might you counteract this?

- What practices of devotion can deepen your trust in God?

SECOND SUNDAY OF LENT
Readings:
Gen 15:5–12, 17–18; Ps 27:1, 7–9, 13–14;
Phil 3:17—4:1; Luke 9:28b–36

YOU'LL NEVER BELIEVE WHAT I SAW!

What would you do if you witnessed a phenomenon in the heavens such as has been reported at Fatima or Lourdes or Medjugorje? Would you fall down on your knees? Or would you turn away in disbelief? Even skeptics are often mesmerized by what they cannot explain. We profess faith in the power of God and in the possibility of a manifestation of that power, and yet many of us are too sophisticated to believe that it might actually happen. Others of us overlook traces of divine revelation in the ordinary events of life.

Today's readings recount extraordinary displays of divine self-revelation. Scholars agree that the accounts themselves may include some degree of exaggerated description; however, this does not discount their profound theological significance. Nor should we be upset to discover that the events might not have happened in exactly the way they are described. The question that should be asked at Fatima or Lourdes or Medjugorje, or by Abram or the disciples of Jesus, is the same in each case: "What does this mean?"

The first reading tells of God's promises to Abram and the covenant made between the two of them. The ritual of "cutting the covenant" was an acted-out curse, signifying the agreed-upon fate of either partner who might be unfaithful to the pact. It meant: "If I violate this pact in any way, you have the right to do to me what we have just done to these animals." Cutting a covenant was serious business. An aspect of the reading, often lost because it seems to be so matter-of-fact, is God's self-revelation: "I am the LORD." In whatever way the event occurred, Abram and his descendants after him were confident of God's special concern and faithful care, regardless of how this and other events of their history unfolded.

This story leaves doubt in no one's mind as to the origin of the covenant relationship. It was unconditionally initiated by God, who had chosen and called Abram in the first place. In like manner, God seeks us much more insistently than we could ever seek God. Our role, like that of Abram, is to accept the favors that are offered us. These favors are really quite ordinary: descendants and a land in which to live. Furthermore, the covenant ritual was probably a well-known cultural practice. In other words, God attends to the very ordinary aspects of our lives and touches us in ways that we will understand.

The account of Jesus' transfiguration describes one moment when the disciples closest to him glimpsed his true identity and the glory that was his. Here too we have an instance of divine revelation. The voice from heaven identifies Jesus as "my chosen Son." Moses and Elijah, who represent the law and the prophets, respectively, discuss the events that Jesus will soon have to face in

Jerusalem. Who would not share Peter's desire to remain in the midst of such a glorious experience?

Though this account describes the glorification of Jesus, its primary focus is his suffering and death. The fact that Moses and Elijah discuss it with Jesus well in advance of its occurrence shows that it was not some dreadful accident of fate. Rather, in some way it brings to fulfillment the essence of Israelite tradition. The presence of Moses and Elijah testifies to this. The transfiguration demonstrates the glorious value of Jesus' suffering and death.

This story reminds us that the extent of God's love for us is revealed in the suffering and death of Jesus, which, though painted in hues of defeat and disgrace, really present the image of unimaginable victory and glory. Realizing this, we must learn to look behind the faces of those who suffer defeat and disgrace in order to find there the unrecognized face of Jesus.

Finally, Paul speaks of a kind of transfiguration that occurs in those who accept Christ. They become conformed to him. And what might this look like? Paul risks being considered arrogant when he instructs the Philippians to be "imitators of me, brothers and sisters, and observe those who thus conduct themselves according to the model you have in us." In other words, God is revealed to us though the goodness of others.

This certainly has been our experience. We all know people whose lives are extraordinary examples of unquestionable integrity, unselfish service of others, generosity, and dependability. Usually, such people will not even recognize the glory that shines forth from them. They will insist that they are only living ordinary lives, and they probably are. It is the way in which they are living these lives, however, that makes them so extraordinary.

Today's readings describe the glory of God as revealed to a wandering migrant, to newly converted pagans, and to simple fishermen, all living lives that were quite ordinary. The accounts remind us that God is revealed to us as well. The challenge today is the same as it always was. We must have eyes that see beyond what we usually see.

Praying with Scripture

- How significant to you is the covenant relationship with God that was established at the time of your baptism?

- How has the glory of God been revealed in your own life?

- In what ways does the good example of others call you to live more faithfully?

THIRD SUNDAY OF LENT
Readings:
Exod 3:1–8a, 13–15; Ps 103:1–4, 6–8, 11;
1 Cor 10:1–6, 10–12; Luke 13:1–9

WHAT DO YOU MAKE OF IT?

Those of us who were raised on some kind of catechism, whether it was the pre–Vatican II *Baltimore Catechism*, the *Dutch Catechism* that was popular during the 1960s and 1970s, or today's *Catechism of the Catholic Church*, were introduced to a list of characteristics identified as attributes of God. This included such clearly articulated traits as: all-present; all-knowing; all-loving, and so on. While the meaning of these characteristics is quite clear, when it comes right down to it, we must admit that we really have very little understanding of the nature of God. Today's readings reconfirm this. Each reading in its own way reminds us that God and the ways of God are truly mysterious.

In the first reading's account of Moses' experience, God's awesomeness is highlighted, both in the description of a bush that was ablaze but not consumed and in the mysterious name that God communicated to the dumbfounded Moses. How could that extraordinary bush possibly be explained? It was certainly meant to catch and hold Moses' attention, and to alert him to the fact that he would never be able to comprehend fully what he was about to experience.

40

And what of the divine name? Scholars agree that it is some form of the Hebrew verb *to be*, but they are not in agreement as to which form. Is it "I am who am," or "I will be who I will be"? And even those who agree on the precise verb form do not all agree on its meaning. Is God claiming to be the source of all that is? Is God saying something about the future? Or is the very ambiguity of its meaning a way of reminding Moses and those after him who claim to know the divine name that God is indeed a mystery that will never be understood? This is a God who reveals and conceals at the same time. The gospel accounts of the Galileans killed by Pilate and the people who were crushed when the tower fell on them illustrate our inability to understand why God allows certain events to occur. The parable of the fig tree does not throw light on this conundrum either. Instead, it points to the need to trust in divine mercy, even in those situations we cannot explain.

Few of us will have a burning bush experience, but all of us have struggled to understand why tragedy seems to fall on innocent people. Just within the recent past we have learned of hundreds of people being swept away by raging waters; we have witnessed entire neighborhoods ravaged by fire or destroyed by war. What did these people do to deserve this? While such a question is understandable, it does arise from a rather mechanistic view of the world. Certainly in some situations what we experience is indeed the consequence of our actions. Becoming ill from eating the wrong kinds of food is an example of this. There is much in life, however, that cannot be traced back to anything we might have done or omitted. So, what are we to do in the face of such ambiguity? The readings offer two major admonitions. In the gospel, Jesus twice calls his listeners to repent, to reform their lives. If we follow this admonition, will it guarantee our safety? Not necessarily, but the parable of the fig tree offers us a second admonition, namely, to trust in the mercy of God.

Paul too insists on these two attitudes of mind and heart. He tells the Corinthians that the fate of the religious ancestors who suffered in the wilderness should be an example to them. Though sustained by God, they sinned nonetheless. Paul exhorts his converts to be faithful and not to presume that membership in the community of believers will automatically save them. They are required to live righteous lives and to rely on Christ who is their true rock of safety.

This is really all that we can do. We do not understand the working of God, and so we are called to trust that, as the great Jewish philosopher Martin Buber taught, God is with us and God is on our side. When faced with tragedy and hardship, we may wonder about this. It is at times like these that we must confess with the psalmist: "Merciful and gracious is the LORD, / slow to anger and abounding in kindness. / For as the heavens are high above the earth, / so surpassing is his kindness toward those who fear him."

This prayer may require tremendous faith and trust in God—religious sentiments that Moses was expected to have. He was called from the relatively trouble-free task of tending the flock of his father-in-law to assume the role of opponent of the pharaoh and leader of a group of escaping, homeless people. Real faith and trust in God are seldom easy to attain and foster. And yet, our God, though utterly mysterious, is truly "kind and merciful" (Ps 103: 8a).

Praying with Scripture

- In what ways have you been faced with the incomprehensibility of God? What has been your response?

- In what areas of your life are your faith and trust in God most challenged? How do you respond?

- How have you experienced God's mercy?

FOURTH SUNDAY OF LENT
Readings:
Josh 5:9a, 10–12; Ps 34:2–7;
2 Cor 5:17–21; Luke 15:1–3, 11–32

REJOICE!

It may seem strange that in the middle of Lent we are told to rejoice. The reason for this is not that we might have a breather from the rigors of penance. (How many of us are really even experiencing any rigors?) Rather, this moment of rejoicing fittingly follows the fundamental theme found in the readings for the other Sundays of this season, that theme being the goodness of God. The versicle for the responsorial psalm might be used as a response to each of the three readings: "Taste and see the goodness of the Lord" (Ps 34: 9a).

In the first reading, we are reminded of how God cared for the Israelites while they were in the wilderness. They had accused God of bringing them out of Egypt so that they might die of hunger in the wilderness. And how did God respond? With punishment? No! The reading tells us that God fed them with mysterious bread that they called manna. The people of Joshua's time had at last arrived in the land of promise. They had been delivered from the reproach of Egypt, and they were now enjoying the produce of the land. They celebrated Passover in memory of God's graciousness to them and to their ancestors. Their celebration was a way of rejoicing.

Paul tells the Corinthian converts that they are a new creation, made so through the blood of Christ. It was the unbounded love of God that was manifested in Christ. In a similar manner, it was the unbounded love of Christ, symbolized by the shedding of his blood, that had reconciled them with God and made them righteous. This is certainly reason to rejoice. In this reading, they do not offer sacrifice as did the Israelites of Joshua's time. Instead, the Corinthians are directed to act as agents of reconciliation throughout the entire world. In this way, they shared in God's plan of salvation.

The gospel reading is one of the best-known and most striking examples of divine graciousness. Though traditionally known as the parable of the prodigal son, it describes the prodigality of the father. He is the one who seems to go to extremes in showering gifts on his repentant son. The theme of reconciliation, so prominent in the passage from Paul, is certainly evident here. It is the father, who in this parable represents God, who takes steps to be reconciled not only with the wayward son but also with the one who was dependable but unforgiving. As the loving father insists: "We must celebrate and rejoice."

In the responsorial psalm we see the psalmist's profound gratitude to God, and we hear the way this gratitude is expressed in rejoicing and praise. Having been delivered from fear, the psalmist both praises God and urges others to turn to God so that they too might be delivered and then praise God. Thus, the psalmist is acting as an agent of reconciliation.

As the author of 2 Timothy tells us: "All scripture is inspired by God and is useful for teaching, for refutation, for correction, and for training in righteousness" (3:16). What lessons might we learn from today's readings? The first and most important lesson to be learned is that of gratitude. There is so much for which each one of us should be grateful. Like the Israelites of old, we have been blessed with freedom and self-determination, the prosperity of the good earth, the love of friends and family. There is so much besides this, so much more that each one in her or his heart cannot even begin to recount God's graciousness.

Like the Corinthians, we have been made a new creation; we have been given a second chance, in fact, many second chances; we have been called by God to continue God's own work of reconciliation. In some ways, this is a very difficult blessing to appreciate. Freedom and food are tangible and we can easily be grateful for them. But few of us really grasp the notion of being a new creation with the responsibility of changing our way of living. The real reason for this may be that we are generally quite satisfied with our approach to life. Furthermore, we normally leave the task of reconciliation to religious or political negotiators. The challenge of this teaching may not yet have touched our minds and hearts.

Like the wayward son who never lost his father's love, we have never really lost God's love; we have been forgiven. We have experienced God's forgiveness whenever our friends, family members, or co-workers have forgiven us our selfishness or impatience. We do understand this kind of reconciliation, and we are usually grateful for it. Sometimes we even celebrate it.

This Sunday is set aside for us to recall God's graciousness and to rejoice because of it. In many ways we have been dead, but through God's grace we have come to life again; we have been lost, but have now been found. We have every reason to rejoice.

Praying with Scripture

- Spend some time reflecting on God's goodness in your life.

- Use the responsorial psalm as a prayer of gratitude.

- How can you act as an agent of God's reconciliation in your family? In your community? In the world?

FIFTH SUNDAY OF LENT
Readings:
Isa 43:16–21; Ps 126:1–6;
Phil 3:8–14; John 8:1–11

"SIN NO MORE!"

The story of the woman taken in adultery raises several questions. We might first ask: "How does a person commit adultery alone? Where is the man?" The fact that only the woman was apprehended is an example of the gender bias of Jesus' adversaries. The compassion of Jesus toward this endangered woman is an example of his disregard for such bias. It is probably not by accident that the story is about a woman, and there is more here than gender bias. All of the gospels depict Jesus as especially sensitive to the needs of poor and disadvantaged people, those who

have been pushed to the margins of the community. Such treatment was particularly true of women in patriarchal societies.
Therefore, the person who stood in shame in the midst of these
men was not only guilty of violating marital trust, but she was a
marginalized woman. She was doubly vulnerable. This fact serves
to heighten Jesus' compassion.

It is clear that the scribes and Pharisees were less interested
in upholding the Law of Moses than they were in trapping Jesus.
They used the woman to try to accomplish this. They reasoned
that if Jesus agreed to her stoning, he would be seen to be as
bloodthirsty as were these "righteous" men. If he protested her
execution, he would be opposing Mosaic Law. They had him over
a barrel. Or so they thought.

We do not know for sure what Jesus wrote on the ground,
but that little detail certainly adds a bit of suspense to the story. It
was his spoken words that caught everyone unaware: "Let the one
among you who is without sin be the first to throw a stone at her."
Now he had them over the barrel. According to Jewish custom,
the eldest should have begun the stoning. Here the elders were the
first to depart. All her accusers gave up their challenge of Jesus.
By walking away, they virtually dismissed the case against the
woman. They had shamed the woman, treating her as a ploy to
trap Jesus. Instead, without minimizing her sinfulness, Jesus
showed her the respect she deserved as a human being, treating
her with compassion. He did not disregard the Law for he
exhorted her: "Do not sin any more." Clearly, he valued repentance and conversion more than just reprisal.

This woman represents all of the people we may have rele-
gated to the margins of society, not merely because we do not
approve of their life-styles, but because for some reason or other we
consider them socially unacceptable. They may not measure up to
our standards because of their racial or ethnic origin, class or economic status, religious or political affiliation, and so on. We may
disdain them because they are too liberal, or too conservative, or too
idiosyncratic. Jesus' love was extended to all, regardless of their
social status. In imitation of him, so must our love extend to all.

This episode is a concrete example of what Isaiah describes
in the first reading: "I am doing something new!" And what is the
"something new" that God does? We are granted a way out of the

deserts of our lives; we are sustained by living waters; we are rescued from the jaws of ravenous beasts. We are forgiven, and we are saved from our own sinfulness. This is what the first reading promises; this is what the gospel reading reports.

All this Lent we have reflected on the marvelous goodness of God in our lives. The theme of God's steadfast love culminates on this Sunday before Holy Week. Both the psalm verses and the reading from Paul direct us to respond to such divine graciousness with joy and gratitude. We have been brought back from captivity, and we are filled with joy; God has done great things for us, and we are filled with joy. Paul, himself a forgiven sinner, has been completely transformed by his faith in Christ Jesus. His life is an example of the gospel exhortation: "Do not sin any more." He left his former life behind as he launched out into the "something new" that God had in store for him, and he did it with no regret.

On this Fifth Sunday of Lent, we stand on the brink of Holy Week, the time set apart for us to reflect seriously on the ultimate realization of God's compassionate love for us. The readings remind us that we cannot stand self-righteously and condemn the lives of others when God is calling them tenderly to conversion. We cannot cling to the past, which may be so comfortable and even socially acceptable, when God is "doing something new" in us. We live in a world that desperately needs "something new." This wondrous newness of God will be born out of conversion, not coercion; it will spring from repentance, not reprisal. It will take shape in the councils of the world, in the boardrooms of the workplace, at the tables of families. We are all called not to "sin any more."

Praying with Scripture

- Is there someone whom you have cut out of your life? Might that person or those people deserve another chance?

- With today's responsorial psalm as your guide, reflect on God's graciousness to you.

- What might you do to enable "something new" to take shape in your life?

PALM SUNDAY OF THE LORD'S PASSION

Readings:
Isa 50:4–7; Ps 22:8–9, 17–20, 23–24;
Phil 2:6–11; Luke 22:14—23:56

WHAT DOES IT MEAN?

As we approach Holy Week we are often inundated with pictures of a bloodied Jesus. Without in any way dismissing the concerns raised by media presentations of Jesus' agony, the passion readings themselves do not concentrate on the details of Jesus' suffering. In fact, there are only three brief explicit references to it in the account of the passion read today: "His sweat became like drops of blood" (Luke 22:44); "The men who held Jesus in custody were…beating him" (22:63); "They crucified him" (23:33). Biblical references to Jesus' passion seem to be more focused on its effects in our lives than on specifics of the passion itself.

Perhaps the best way to understand the message of today's readings is to place them within the context of Paul's hymn of praise of Christ Jesus as found in the Letter to the Philippians. Paul does not sketch a graphic account of Jesus' agony, but neither does he minimize it. His report interprets the suffering: Jesus emptied himself; he took the form of a slave; he humbled himself; he became obedient even to death on the cross. Paul identifies Jesus as a man who knew suffering, but he does not portray him as a mere helpless victim. According to Paul, Jesus emptied himself of all divine prerogatives; his torturers sought to empty him of all human dignity. His deliberate self-emptying, however, allowed them to apprehend him. Though he suffered, he did not relinquish his dignity. Jesus was in the form of God; their brutal treatment left him deformed. But he freely took the form of a slave, and so it was his choice to be physically broken. Jesus humbled himself; they set out to humiliate him. Here again, it was his choice. Jesus was obedient to his destiny; they thought that they were putting an end to him.

The reading from Isaiah is the third of four pieces of poetry known as the Servant Songs. Here the "servant of the LORD" tells us that he was called by God to speak words of comfort to the weary. Some resented this, and so they assaulted him. In the face of it, he did not defend himself, but continued to trust in God. Early Christians easily identified Jesus with this servant. Jesus too preached to the needy; for this he too was assaulted; neither did he defend himself, but trusted in God throughout the entire ordeal.

Psalm 22 is a combination of a lament and a hymn of praise. The psalmist complains of having to endure ridicule and of being attacked. Complaint is followed by a prayer of trust and a petition for help. The psalm ends with a promise of praise and a call to others to praise God. As bitter as the suffering may have been, the psalmist does not end this prayer on a note of despair. Rather, praise implies that the psalmist is certain that God will answer that prayer. For this reason, praise is appropriate, even in the midst of suffering.

The two readings and the psalm all begin with suffering but end with trust. The proclamation from Paul goes even further than trust, ending with the exaltation of Jesus. These passages set the context within which we should consider the passion. They do not minimize the bitter rejection that Jesus faced or the excruciating suffering that he endured, but they do assure us that there is more here than meets the eye. Jesus' sacrifice was the price he paid for being faithful to his calling.

As for the passion narrative itself, the sobering details of the story point out how easy it is for any one of us to sacrifice genuine integrity. Judas is not the only one who ever betrayed a friend, nor is Peter alone in protecting himself at the expense of another. Many of us know how easy it is for those in positions of authority to sacrifice an individual for what they consider the best interests of the group. Religious leaders, convinced of their own legitimacy, are known to silence any opposing voice. Finally, we should not underestimate the force of crowd mentality. It is so easy to join it and lose our own sense of justice in the process, or to be so frightened by the crowd that we fail to stand by those who might become its victims. There is enough culpability here to go around.

Let us enter into the passion of Jesus in a way that will move us toward genuine conversion and transformation. Let us recognize our own strengths or limitations in the characters of the story and note how Jesus calls them to greater fidelity. Let us identify with Jesus. He willingly set aside privilege for the sake of others; he remained true to his calling, despite the cost that was exacted; he refused to meet violence with violence. Through it all, Jesus remained tenaciously faithful to God and lovingly open to all others. The readings of this Sunday set these challenges before us.

Praying with Scripture

- What effect has the suffering of Jesus had on your life?

- Where do you see hope in the suffering of the world?

- What have you done to alleviate the sufferings of one other person?

Easter Season

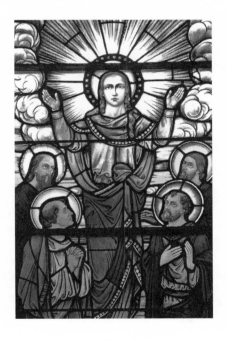

EASTER SUNDAY (C)
Readings:
Acts 10:34a, 37–43; Ps 118:1–2, 16–17, 22–23;
Col 3:1–4; John 20:1–9

WHAT HAPPENED?

If we who profess faith in the resurrection of the body were to visit a grave and find it open and the body gone, we would most likely assume that it had been taken by someone. It is no wonder that Mary, Peter, and John drew that same conclusion when they arrived at Jesus' tomb. After all, dead bodies don't just get up and walk away.

Everyone is interested in what happened to the body of Jesus, but there is no biblical account that tells us. All we know is that his followers found that the tomb was empty, and some people claimed to have seen Jesus afterward. Today's readings refer to both of these details. The gospel passage focuses on the empty tomb; Peter's speech recorded in the first reading states that the Risen Lord was visible to the disciples. These traditions are less interested in details of the resurrection itself than in what it meant and continues to mean to us.

Peter traces the life of Jesus all the way to his death and resurrection. His purpose is to show that this man Jesus was "the one appointed by God as judge of the living and the dead." He was God's chosen one, the one through whom fulfillment appeared. If anyone claimed such an exalted position and died, the claim would most likely die with that person. But to make the claim, die, and then rise from the dead gave legitimation to that claim. On what grounds did Peter make such claims? The very life and the teaching of Jesus made them. Now that he was raised from the dead, those who witnessed his life and death were commissioned to give witness to his resurrection. We may not know what happened to Jesus, but we can see what happened to those witnesses. They fearlessly preached what initially they had not understood.

Paul's teaching about the resurrection focuses on Christ's exaltation at the right hand of God. Here too Paul is less interested in how Jesus reached God's right hand than in the implications of the resurrection and exaltation for the lives of Christians. Paul maintains that those who are joined to Christ die with Christ to this life, are raised with Christ to a life with God, and will eventually share in the glory of Christ's exaltation.

The sequence of the theological issues found in today's readings is liturgical rather than chronological. In other words, at first the followers of Jesus lacked understanding of what had happened, as recounted in today's gospel. Only later did preachers like Peter and Paul give testimony to their faith in the resurrection. What happened that changed them? It was probably an experience of the Risen Lord. This answer throws us back to the initial question: What happened?

Skeptics demand proof that Jesus rose from the dead. The readings for today provide us with three places to look for proof. The first is the fact that the tomb was empty. But this is questionable evidence, because the empty tomb simply means that the body of Jesus was gone, not that he was risen. The second evidence is the resurrection appearances. This is also rather weak evidence, because the authenticity of mystical experience is very difficult to prove. Though it is questionable as proof, at least an empty tomb is concrete. While it may be even weaker evidence, a personal experience is real to the one experiencing it, but only to that one.

The third place to look for evidence of the resurrection is the least concrete, but probably the most reliable. It is found in the quality of the lives of those who live out their faith in the resurrection. We see this clearly in the transformation of Peter, who went from misunderstanding the scriptures to interpreting them through the lens of the resurrection. We see it also in Paul, who had set out to put Christians to death, only to become the champion of "dying and rising with Christ."

We see what happened in the lives of countless women and men today who are examples of extraordinary integrity in the midst of deceit, examples of dedicated service in a world of selfishness, of patience and understanding in the face of violence, and of forgiveness and reconciliation where there has been personal violation. Such lives are evidence that Jesus has risen from the dead and is alive in the world today.

So what are we to make of this wondrous day? How are we to understand the mystery it sets before us? This is the day on which we celebrate the fact of faith that Jesus was willing to die for us but was not willing to stay dead. By rising, he shattered the hold that death had over all of us. It couldn't keep him down. And if we are joined to him, neither can it keep us down. We are Easter people when we put on new lives, not merely new clothes. By the grace of God, someday the power of Easter will so transform us that people will wonder: What happened?

Praying with Scripture

- In what ways does your life give concrete evidence of the truth of the resurrection?

- What new life does this feast invite you to put on?

- Spend some time reflecting on the challenge found in the reading from Colossians.

SECOND SUNDAY OF EASTER
Readings:
Acts 5:12–16; Ps 118:2–4, 13–15, 22–24; Rev 1:9–11a, 12–13, 17–19; John 20:19–31

I HAVE TO SEE IT MYSELF!

There is an old saying: "I'm from Missouri, you have to show me." This does not mean that Missourians are slow to learn. Rather, it means that they do not easily take someone's word without some form of verification. They are not unique in this characteristic. Actually, many of us are very much like the

Missourians; we too want concrete evidence before we are willing to accept certain claims. Those who share these somewhat skeptical sentiments have a patron saint in the apostle Thomas. Though he is sometimes referred to as "doubting Thomas," he was not a man without faith. He did believe. It was just that he was unwilling to accept the resurrection of Jesus on the word of the other disciples. He wanted concrete proof; he wanted to see for himself and to touch the wounds. How can we blame him? No one really expected that Jesus would rise from the dead. It seems to have come as a surprise to everyone. As for Thomas, after his experience of the Risen Lord, his enthusiastic testimony was a remarkable declaration of faith in Christ's divinity. He cried out: "My Lord and my God!"

Generally speaking, our faith comes to us through the words of others. We hear these words at home, in school, at church, and from people in many corners of our lives. If we ever challenge certain aspects of the faith, it is usually because we judge them to be irrelevant. Thomas, on the other hand, was skeptical about what was told to him because he thought that the message was too good to be true. In comparison, we may be so familiar with the news of the resurrection that we cease to be amazed by it. If this is the case, then we certainly need a patron saint like Thomas.

The readings for the Sundays after Easter are meant to serve as catechesis or religious instruction, primarily for the newly baptized, but we all can benefit from this teaching as well. There are several lessons in the readings for today. The first concerns our responsibility for handing on the religious tradition that has been handed down to us. As Christians, we are all called to this responsibility, regardless of our age, occupation, or state in life. How is this to be done? Actually, in ways that are quite simple. We hand it on through our teaching, whether it is done formally or informally; we proclaim its message as we live out its ethical values. What we say and how we act exclaim to those around us: "We have seen the Lord."

A second lesson to be learned today concerns the role that the Christian community plays in our lives. Community-based societies, such as those described in the Bible, are well aware of the importance of belonging to a group. Membership gives these people identity, meaning, and support. Today's readings confirm this. There is a communal dimension to every resurrection appearance of Jesus. In fact, Thomas's predicament was the result of his having been absent from the community of disciples when Jesus appeared to them. In the first reading, while Peter is a prominent figure in the action that is described, the miracles were actually performed by all of the apostles. God's concern is for the entire people. We who live in a society that values an exaggerated form of individualism have much to learn about being members of the body of Christ.

The first reading for today provides us with yet another lesson. It illustrates how the power of the resurrection working through ordinary people can bring about miracles. Some might think that this is too bold a claim. And yet a friendly smile, a gentle touch, a willingness to forgive have healed more than one broken spirit; and the challenging words of a parent, a teacher, or a friend have quickened many minds and hearts. We have all witnessed such miracles with our own eyes. We ourselves may have even been touched by them. Then why are we so afraid to believe that we can make a difference in our world?

In the reading from Revelation, the visionary named John describes an extraordinary experience he had while living in banishment in the penal colony on the island of Patmos. It should be noted that not even incarceration could prevent the spread of the gospel. John's days of preaching might have been over, but he could write and write he did. The scene described in the passage is of extraordinary splendor, and there in the midst of that splendor was "one like a son of man." Presumably this figure was the Risen Christ. The message is even more astounding than the vision itself. Death has been overcome; Jesus the Christ is now alive forever. It is the very message that Thomas found so hard to accept at first. It is the message that we are called to live out in our lives so that through us others will be able to exclaim: "We have seen the Lord."

Praying with Scripture

- Thomas was transformed by faith in the resurrection. What has your faith done for you?

- What do you do that strengthens the communities of which you are a member?

- In what ways might you effect change in your world?

THIRD SUNDAY OF EASTER
Readings:
Acts 5:27–32, 40b–41; Ps 30:2, 4–6, 11–13;
Rev 5:11–14; John 21:1–19

IS HE ALIVE IN US?

Not too many people serve fried fish for breakfast—maybe smoked, but not fried. But who would turn down such a breakfast if Jesus were the one offering it? Still, a breakfast of bread and fish? On the other hand, it was not unlike the meal Jesus earlier served to the large crowd on the mountainside (John 6:9–11). Both times he astonished the disciples with the meal. Unfortunately we may know these stories so well that they no longer astonish us anymore. If this is the case, then we may not really understand them after all.

This Easter season provides us with readings that all focus on some aspect of the resurrection. Today we consider two dimensions of this mystery, namely, the wondrous character of the Risen Lord, and the effect our own transformed lives can have on the lives of others. In the vision recounted in the reading from Revelation, the visionary John was transported to the heavenly throne room where angels, four living creatures resembling a lion, a calf, a human being, and an eagle, respectively, and twenty-four elders all pay homage to "the Lamb that was slain." This Lamb, who is none other than the Risen Lord himself, has been invested in "power and riches, wisdom and strength, / honor and glory and blessing."

The gospel passage recounts how the same Risen Lord revealed himself to his disciples at the Sea of Tiberias. After an entire night on the water, these seasoned fishermen had caught nothing. Then a mysterious man on shore told them where to cast their nets. For a reason not given in the text, they obeyed him, and their catch was such that they were unable to pull it in. It was only after this marvel that one of their number recognized Jesus and cried out: "It is the Lord." The disciples knew that Jesus had died, but there he was, alive and serving them breakfast. One has to wonder, after he rose from the dead, why did he linger on earth? Why not return to God and leave these fishermen to resume the occupation to which they had already returned? No, the Risen Lord had something else in mind for them. He first fed those awestruck men, and then instructed them to "feed my lambs....Tend my sheep....Feed my sheep."

It is a sobered Peter whom we find in this account. Gone is the bravado he demonstrated when, before Jesus' capture by the authorities, his passion and death, Peter insisted that he would lay down his life for Jesus (John 13:37). Though Jesus' interrogation of Peter is quite moving, three times Jesus forces Peter to declare humbly his love for his Lord. This probably corresponded to Peter's threefold denial of even knowing Jesus (13:38). The passage ends with a prediction of Peter's future death. Mention of his being bound could well refer to the practice of binding the hands of the one to be crucified. Having been given the role of shepherd, once held by Jesus, Peter is now told that he will suffer a fate similar to that which Jesus suffered.

In the reading from Acts of the Apostles, we see the importance of both teaching the good news and witnessing to the resurrection of Jesus. The disciples of Jesus were following the commission they had received from him. When given orders to desist from their teaching, they refused to obey, despite the suffering that such disregard of the High Priest's orders brought upon them. They continued to teach concerning those marvels to which they had been witnesses. We all teach; some formally, others informally. And we all give witness by the way we live. Though the gospel account states that the commission to leadership is directed to Peter, we know that others shared in that ministry as well. This is also true today. Some do in fact carry the heavy burden of church leadership, but they do not carry it alone. Parish councils, directors of educational, liturgical, or other pastoral ministries all share in the care of the flock of Jesus.

If the stories about the Risen Lord no longer astonish us, the implications of the resurrection in our lives very well may. It is not enough to proclaim: "I believe!" We have all been called to witness to that faith. Whether we realize it or not, our daily lives cry out as loudly as did the preaching of the apostles. This witness includes the ways we interact with family members and neighbors, with companions in the workplace and sales personnel with whom we interact, even with strangers on the bus or train. Faith in the resurrection of Jesus influences the decisions that we make about everything in life. It prompts us to share what we have, not merely to store it up; to be honest, rather than deceitful; to respect others, rather than manipulate them; to forgive, rather than hold grudges. Jesus extends the invitation to us that he extended to Peter: "Follow me." Our manner of living reveals how we have responded to that invitation.

Praying with Scripture

- How does your manner of living proclaim that Jesus is alive in you?

- In what ways might you follow Jesus' injunction to "feed my sheep"?

- Make today's responsorial psalm your prayer today.

FOURTH SUNDAY OF EASTER
Readings:
Acts 13:14, 43–52; Ps 100:1–3, 5;
Rev 7:9, 14b–17; John 10:27–30

A GREAT AND DIVERSE MULTITUDE!

Today is traditionally known as Good Shepherd Sunday. It provides an opportunity for us to reflect on God's loving care for us, the kind of unselfish care that a shepherd shows a cherished flock of sheep. The readings, however, call our attention to the flock rather than to the shepherd. Nonetheless, the character of the flock does tell us something about the one who guides and cares for it. For example, the fact that there are different kinds of sheep indicates that the shepherd values diversity. Despite this diversity, there is still only one flock, not two or more. Therefore, unity within this diversity is another value found in the readings.

Though the gospel passage is short, it provides us with a clear sketch of Jesus as a caring shepherd. His words tell us that the sheep are his, given to him by the one he calls Father. Not only are they his property, but they also share a relationship of intimacy with him. He knows them, and they know him. When he calls out to them, they hear his voice, and they follow him. Under his protection they are secure, for he promises that "they shall never perish." This is very reassuring, particularly in a world that seldom can ensure security of any kind.

The diversity within the community of believers is seen in the other two readings. In the passage from Acts of the Apostles we read that Paul and Barnabas moved the fledgling church into the realm of the Gentiles, where many new converts are made. Bringing Gentiles into the embrace of the community of believers was not accomplished without opposition and struggle. Some of the Jews resented the success of these two disciples, and they caused difficulty for the apostles. This did not deter them from their goal, however. "Both Paul and Barnabas spoke out boldly....The Gentiles were delighted when they heard this and glorified the word of the Lord." The fearlessness of these two men resulted in the spread of the gospel and an increase in the membership of the Christian community.

The reading from the Book of Revelation provides a picture of this community growth and the diversity of its membership. We see a great multitude standing before the Lamb, a multitude consisting of those "from every nation, race, people, and tongue." They have all been saved by the sacrificial blood of the Lamb, who is Christ the Lord. Here too we find the metaphor of the shepherd. The victorious Lamb whose blood was shed is characterized as a shepherd who will lead believers "to springs of life-giving water."

The notion of unity in diversity is quite popular today, at least as a socio-religious slogan. In fact, however, unity in diversity is a very difficult balance to achieve. Most of us tend to associate with people with whom we share racial, cultural, economic, religious, or ideological characteristics and values. At times we may even ridicule those who appear to be different. This was not at all the attitude shared by Paul and Barnabas. They deliberately ventured out into the land of the Gentiles, there to spread the good news of the gospel. Furthermore, we know that those Gentiles who embraced the faith were not required to accept all of the religious practices cherished by the Jewish Christians. This means that from the very first days of the Christian movement, there was a degree of unity in diversity. This characteristic marked the church from its foundation and even down to our own day. The diversity within the church of which we are a part is evidence of this.

The Good Shepherd is committed to the well-being of us all, people "from every nation, race, people, and tongue." Unlike the societies in which we live, the genuine differences among us in this community remain as distinctions marking us all as unique, not as separations that keep us apart. They actually add to the color and texture of the community of believers, rather than alienate or marginalize us. We are all God's people, "the flock he tends," and there is no dominant or superior group within it.

Today's readings present the Risen Lord as both the Good Shepherd and the Lamb that was slain. Actually, he is the Good Shepherd in virtue of his being the victorious Lamb, for he paid for the undisputed right to lead us by the shedding of his blood. If we hear his voice and follow him, he will lead us also to springs of living water, and he will wipe away every tear from our eyes. Over the years we have come to accept the fact of diversity within the Christian community. What were once ethnic parishes have become multicultural communities of faith. We have come to appreciate the diversity among us, rather than try to stamp it out. We are indeed a great and diverse multitude, all sheep of the same Good Shepherd. This is reason enough to cry out: "Alleluia!"

Praying with Scripture

- Which people have you kept at a distance because of their different origin, race, or tongue? How might you change this?

- Pray for the grace to hear the voice of the Good Shepherd and to follow wherever he leads you.

- In what ways might you act as a guide for others?

FIFTH SUNDAY OF EASTER
Readings:
Acts 14:21–27; Ps 145:8–13;
Rev 21:1–5a; John 13:31–33a, 34–35

WHAT'S NEW?

We seem to tire so easily of the ordinary in life. Many of us are constantly looking for something new, something exciting. We want to be entertained by life and to have the latest of everything, whether that means style, electronic equipment, or fame. We are often taken in by the advertisements that insist: "This is *really new*, and you can't live without it!"

Advertisers are not the first to make such claims. Nor are they completely misleading. We are certainly living in times of rapid change. In many cases, we purchase an item one week and there is a new and improved version the next. Furthermore, it is often extremely difficult to live, much less advance, without some contemporary devices. We are always faced with questions such as: "How new and improved does everything have to be?" "What can I really live without?"

The readings for today make precisely this claim: "This is *really new*, and you can't live without it!" But the biblical authors are not talking about something that is merely new and improved today but will probably be replaced tomorrow. When they speak of "a new heaven and a new earth," "a new Jerusalem," or "a new commandment," they are referring to eschatological reality. The Greek word for *new* that is used here indicates the extraordinary character of this newness. This is an act of God.

The reading from Revelation sets the context for our reflections. The vision found there is rich in symbolic language. The new heaven and new earth represent all of reality. Within it we find the new Jerusalem, the people personified as a bride. Marital imagery characterizes the loving union between God and the people. This new reality is a joyous time, a time of unending happiness.

The scene is really a vision of the new age of eschatological fulfillment inaugurated by the death and resurrection of Jesus. When he burst forth from the grave, he completely altered the powers of both heaven and earth. He invited his followers to enter a new Jerusalem where they would dwell with God in their midst. It might be better to say that they would dwell there in the midst of God. This awe-inspiring vision declares that everything has been transformed.

In the gospel reading, Jesus instructs his disciples to "love one another." Here he speaks of *agápē*, a love that requires total commitment and trust. It is the kind of love with which God loves us, a love that should be the model of the love we have for others. When we examine the demands of this love, we realize just how revolutionary it is and what a change in attitude it requires.

Although we may not be called to the same kind of missionary activity as were Paul and Barnabas, we must still be as unselfish in our service of others as were these early Christians. Family life can be very trying, and not all people are exhilarated by the work they do. Still, it is precisely in situations such as these that we might be called to "undergo many hardships."

The new kind of love that Jesus holds out to us might require us to open doors that we have closed against others, to respond to appeals that cry out for our help, to forgive oversights or mistakes of others. This love opens our eyes to facts that we might otherwise overlook, such as the realization that the poor in the world belong to our family; that those who live in despair might be saved by our care of them; that peace can come to the world through our efforts. "This is how all will know that [we] are [his] disciples, if [we] have love for one another."

John's vision of the new heaven and the new earth is in the future only because we have failed to live it in our present. Jesus has risen from the dead, and now all things are new. "The old order has passed away." We have entered the age of fulfillment. If we expect it to be Pollyannaville, we are badly mistaken. Yet, it is within our power to fashion a world, a country, a neighborhood, and a family where there is genuine love for one another and sincere concern for the well-being of all. Our societies do not always foster such unselfishness. That is why people who do live this extraordinary love stand out from the crowd. They might be ridiculed for their manner of living, but they nonetheless show by it that they are God's people and that God does indeed dwell with them.

Shortly after the Second Vatican Council banners appeared with the message: "We are Easter people!" The slogan may not have had a wide appeal, but the challenge that it implies continues to be true. Indeed, we are Easter people. We have been raised with Jesus from the dead, and now no power on earth can really conquer us. Even the primordial forces of chaos and evil, characterized by the raging sea, have been vanquished. What is holding us back from transforming the world?

Praying with Scripture

- Thank God for the people in your life whose love for you has made you a better person.

- How might you manifest such love in your own life?

- To what kind of "new" life is God calling you?

SIXTH SUNDAY OF EASTER
Readings:
Acts 15:1–2, 22–29; Ps 67:2–3, 5–6, 8;
Rev 21:10–14, 22–23; John 14:23–29

HOME ALONE?

In the popular Christmas movie *Home Alone*, an inattentive family goes off on a vacation, oblivious to the absence of one of the children. Left with only his own ingenuity, the young boy fends off a pair of bungling burglars. There are some touching moments in this film, but it basically consists of a series of humorous setbacks that the child wields against the inept intruders. Because we know that the story will have a happy ending, the movie probably does not leave us with the question: "How would I cope if I were left alone?"

In the gospel reading for this Sunday before the ascension, Jesus tells his disciples that he will be leaving them. In a sense, they will be alone. Although he promises to send the Advocate, the Holy Spirit, they will have to fend for themselves, and the enemy or enemies that they will face will not be bunglers. While Jesus was alive, the disciples trusted in his ability to hold opposition at bay. They must have wondered where they would find the strength and direction they would need in his absence. Though he announces his impending departure, he does promise to leave them what they will need to continue. They will have "the Advocate, the Holy Spirit, whom the Father will send in my name"—but they probably do not understand the significance of this promise. It will take their experience on the day of Pentecost to realize the power that they will wield as a result of their being possessed by this Spirit. At this point, all they would know is loss.

Knowing that the advent of the Spirit was in the future, Jesus encouraged his friends with a message of peace: "Peace I leave with you; my peace I give to you." Even this they probably misunderstood. They had known moments of peace, times when they were away from the frenzy of the crowds and the opposition of some of the leaders of the people. But Jesus said that his peace was different. They would have to face the challenges that awaited them before they would be able to grasp the nature of his peace.

The passage from Acts of the Apostles provides us with a sketch of the early Christian community. There we see that Jesus was faithful to his promise; the Holy Spirit was indeed present and active in the life of the church. The disciples had not been left alone. The ministry to the Gentiles had resulted in an increase in membership in the church. In it we find Paul, Barnabas, Judas, Silas, and the Gentile converts, along with the apostles, elders, and the Jewish Christians in Jerusalem. The diversity also spawned dissension and factions, however, and something had to be done lest these differences caused the church to splinter and collapse. But what? A meeting was called, a church council. They would seek the strength and direction of the Holy Spirit working through the church. In this way they arrived at a decision. The announcement of the decision is telling: "It is the decision of the Holy Spirit and of us." The church was clearly not alone.

If we look at this church today simply from a human perspective, all we see are limited women and men. We are people who, left to our own ingenuity, are often bunglers. But we have not been left alone. Jesus promised us the Holy Spirit, and the power of that Spirit has transformed us into the glorious holy city of the new Jerusalem envisioned in the reading from Revelation. The vision that was granted John revealed a city not only magnificent in the splendor of God, but also fortified against intruders. It was a city that included the names of both the twelve tribes of Israel and the twelve apostles of the Lamb, an indication that all people have access to it. The visionary was surprised that there was no temple in the city, until he realized that there was no need of a temple since both the almighty God and the Lamb were present.

This vision is of the church today as well as the church of the future. It is the church that, through the power of the Spirit, we are becoming. As we look around, we might not recognize this church, for today it has been exposed in all its weakness. Not unlike the community described in the reading from Acts, members vigorously disagree over diverse teachings and practices. Rather than enrich the fabric of the church, cultural differences often threaten to tear it apart. This is far from what was intended by Jesus. Fortified by the power of the Holy Spirit, however, we too can live lives of openness and compassion, of forgiveness and commitment. We can indeed make real the peace that Jesus promised. In the community of love, which is the true image of the church, no one is ever alone.

Praying with Scripture

- Do I look to the community of believers for the strength and support I need? If not, why not?

- Does anyone look to me for that strength or support? If not, why not?

- Pray to the Holy Spirit for the insight and the strength needed to live a life of integrity, despite the struggles you must face.

ASCENSION
Readings:
Acts 1:1–11; Ps 47:2–3, 6–9; Eph 1:17–23 (or Heb 9:24–28; 10:19–23); Luke 24:46–53

WHAT DOES IT MEAN?

When I was a child, I often wondered how far up Jesus had to ascend before he got to heaven. Then, as an adult, I was dumbfounded when I read that one of the early Soviet astronauts made a comment about not seeing any traces up in space of the ascended Jesus. It is not that I have a clearer understanding of this mystery than I had as a child or than the astronaut seems to have had. I simply ask different questions now. I don't wonder where he went or where is he now. Instead, I wonder what it all means.

Those who have left us an account of the ascension possessed a prescientific concept of the structure of the cosmos, one that is quite different from ours. Today we speak of the expanding galaxies and curved space-time. The ancients believed in a three-tiered universe, with the realm of the dead literally under the world of the living and heaven literally above it all. When they spoke of Jesus returning to God and being enthroned in heaven, they envisioned this as some kind of ascension into the sky. The comment of the astronaut shows that he held two conflicting perceptions of the universe, an extraordinarily sophisticated one developed by NASA and a prescientific one shaped by a literal reading of the Bible. Many of us today hold the same two world views, though we do not always acknowledge that they conflict. We who have been shaped by the scientific age in which we live want to know what really happened. We are not unlike the disciples who were "standing there looking up to the sky." Today's readings don't explain what happened. Instead, they throw light on what it all means.

The ascension is one aspect of the broader mystery of the resurrection. No longer is Jesus bodily present among his disciples. The church is now living in a new reality. While upcoming readings for Ordinary Time will describe this new reality, today's readings focus on Jesus' exaltation. Easter stories showed Jesus trying to assure his followers that they were really experiencing him and not some illusion. He walked, talked, and ate with them. They came to realize that the one who had died on the cross was now alive. In the readings for today we behold him in all of his divine glory, taking his place in heaven next to God.

The focus of this feast is the heavenly reign of Christ, not the details of the ascension itself. The first reading simply states that "he was lifted up, and a cloud took him from their sight." The reading from the Letter to the Ephesians says that Jesus is at God's "right hand in the heavens." In the gospel passage we read that he "was taken up to heaven." The challenge these readings set before us is spiritual, not scientific. They all declare that Jesus is with God, and that there he is at God's right hand, the place of honor par excellence. So, what does it mean? The reading from Ephesians offers us some insight. It states that God placed Jesus "far above every principality, authority, power, and dominion," most likely references to celestial beings. God also placed "all things beneath his feet," a metaphor of royal rule.

This all means that the ascension of Jesus is a metaphor for his exaltation by God as the victorious ruler over all. Does this mean that he did not go up to heaven? Of course not. That description was the best way people with a three-tiered concept of the universe could explain what they believed. Today, we who live with a big-bang, string-theory understanding of the universe simply speak of it differently.

In the accounts of the ascension read today, the attention of the disciples is redirected from their experience of Jesus to their own responsibilities. In the first reading, Jesus directs his disciples to be his witnesses. Their ministry will begin where they are in Jerusalem, move out from there to the surrounding area of Judea, then to neighboring Samaria, and finally to the ends of the world. They cannot afford to stand around looking up to the sky. They have work to do. The gospel passage contains a similar message. There Jesus instructs the disciples that they will be witnesses to his life, death, and resurrection "to all the nations, beginning from Jerusalem."

The first disciples were faithful to these instructions. They brought the good news of salvation to the ends of the earth. We are evidence of their success. Now it is our turn. We cannot stand looking up to heaven, both astonished and frightened by Jesus' absence from our sight. We have work to do. If Jesus' message is to be brought into the world, it is now up to us to do it. He has been exalted by God, and we must now be his witnesses "to the ends of the earth."

Praying with Scripture

- What does the exaltation of Jesus mean in your life today?
- In what ways do you already witness to the good news of the gospel?
- In what new ways might you witness in the future?

SEVENTH SUNDAY OF EASTER
Readings:
Acts 7:55–60; Ps 97:1–2, 6–7, 9;
Rev 22:12–14, 16–17, 20; John 17:20–26

DREAM THE IMPOSSIBLE DREAM!

We might be tempted to laugh at the naive optimism of Don Quixote who, though considered ridiculous, saw himself as a champion of the vulnerable. But is he really so far removed from us? As children, we may have envisioned ourselves as an astronaut hero, Miss America, or the batter who wins the World Series in the bottom of the ninth inning. As we entered adulthood, we might have settled for the distinction of being the Betty Crocker recipe winner or the "father of the year." Are such dreams really implausible? Someone will eventually win these honors. Why should we feel that we must always settle for less?

Our religious tradition invites us to cling to convictions that might appear to be even more implausible. During this Easter season, we stand in awe of the mystery of the resurrection. Jesus, put to death as a common felon, is raised to life and remains among us to this day. On the feast of the Ascension, we considered one aspect of this mystery, namely, his exaltation with God and our share in his glory. The splendor of this feast overflows into today's readings. Here we behold again the crucified Lord raised to glory. The image is indeed extraordinary!

Whatever Stephen saw in his vision, as related in the first reading, strengthened both his faith in the crucified now-risen Jesus and his resolve to cling to that faith even in the face of death. What Stephen offers us as merely a glimpse is more fully described in the vision reported in the passage from Revelation. This crucified now-glorious Jesus is the beginning and end of all things. Because he has conquered death, he can unreservedly promise us life. "The one who wants it [will] receive the gift of life-giving water." Those joined to him will be energized by the very power that flows from him. Is this an impossible dream?

According to John, the night before he died, Jesus prayed that all of us might share in his future glory. It is precisely through our union with Jesus that this will happen. This is a matter of faith, however. We are called to believe that Jesus was not merely put to death, but that his death and resurrection conquered the stranglehold that death can have over us, and to believe that we can share in his glory. This calls for faith, because it may not appear that his death and resurrection have changed anything in the world. The world still harbors selfishness and arrogance, deceit and abuse, hatred and revenge. Is this vision of triumph and glory implausible?

Our faith tells us that this vision describes what really took place. Yet, can we discover any concrete evidence that confirms its trustworthiness? Yes, we can! But the evidence is not in some vision of heaven; it can be found in the very struggles of human life. Even the religious skeptics are often amazed by the faith that believers demonstrate. This faith has fortified public martyrs and unsung women and men down through the ages. It has been the support of missionaries in far-flung countries, of public protesters who insist that evil can be overturned by the efforts of people of integrity, of grieving parents who continue to believe even as they bury their children.

We so often see such faith in the dignity and unselfishness of people who are forced to endure degradation or poverty; we see it in the generosity of those who work in shelters and soup kitchens; we see it in the commitment of those who teach and proclaim truth, even when it is not popular. The glory of Jesus shines through the marks of his ignominy. Our share in his glory shines through our commitment to others in situations of comparable ignominy.

Stephen's faith in the glorious Jesus and in his own future share in that glory was witnessed by Saul who, at that time, clearly supported the persecution of Christians. But who knows what seeds of faith were being planted in Saul's mind and heart? When Jesus prayed for those who would believe on the word of others, he was praying for you and for me. Our faith came to us and has been strengthened through the words and example of others—our families and teachers, our friends and acquaintances, even people we don't know but who have somehow inspired us. We may not always reflect on this, but this is the way God seems to act.

Another aspect of the mystery of the resurrection must not be ignored. It is the fact that through us the glory of the risen Jesus is revealed to others. This is not naive, quixotic optimism; it is not an impossible dream. It is an aspect of our faith that is both reassuring and challenging, an aspect that is much more significant than any childhood dream or purely human ambition. The character of our lives gives testimony to the glory of Jesus.

Praying with Scripture

- Who in your acquaintance witnesses to life even in the face of death? What might you learn from this?

- What in your experience most threatens your share in resurrection glory?

- Pray that God will give you the strength to withstand this threat.

PENTECOST
Readings:
Acts 2:1–11; Ps 104:1, 24, 29–31, 34;
1 Cor 12:3b–7, 12–13; John 20:19–23

LOOK WHAT BLEW INTO TOWN!

The movement of the winds is a mysterious phenomenon. It cannot be seen, but its effects are constantly around us. In the summer it can be a cooling touch on our sweltering skin, while in the winter it can slap us hard in the face. It carries the seeds that will eventually germinate into new forms of life, yet it can also destroy life and property in the fury of its hurricanes and tornadoes. It has guided many ships across the endless oceans, and it has hurtled others onto rocks that rip them apart. The winds are truly wondrous displays of power.

In the Old Testament, the words for *wind*, *breath*, and *spirit* are often used interchangeably. It is no wonder, then, that the coming of the Spirit of God is characterized in the first reading for today as "a strong driving wind" that "filled the entire house." What must they have thought? Was this a sudden storm? A tornado? Would the house collapse around them, crushing them with its force? But there was no furious wind, only the sound of one. And then tongues of fire, another symbol of the power of God, appeared on each of those in that particular house. Next, they all began to speak in different languages. First the sound of a mighty wind, then a sign of God's presence, and finally a miracle of tongues! What did all of this mean? We are told that they were filled with the Holy Spirit. Did they realize that? They must have realized something because they were now able to act in ways that previously they were incapable of acting.

We are told that at this time "devout Jews from every nation under heaven [were] staying in Jerusalem." They had come to Jerusalem to celebrate the Jewish pilgrim feast of Pentecost that marked the wheat harvest. When they heard the sound of the mighty wind, they gathered outside the house where the disciples were staying, wondering what had taken place. When the disciples came out to them, proclaiming the mighty acts of God, the people were astonished that they each heard the message in his or her native tongue. The Spirit that had transformed the disciples from fearful individuals into bold missionaries was now transforming these people through the words spoken. The miracle of tongues of speech that occurred among the crowds must have been spectacular. Yet there were still more phenomenal marvels that occurred that day.

In the gospel reading we see that the Spirit does not come to the disciples under the guise of a mighty wind as in the first reading. Rather, Jesus breathes on them and that is when they receive the Spirit. Here too it is the power of the Spirit working through them that is important. At this time they are empowered to forgive sin and to hold back forgiveness as well. They are given remarkable powers. Is there a contradiction here? Did the Spirit descend upon the disciples on the night of the resurrection, as recounted in the gospel reading, or fifty days later at Pentecost? As is the case with all of the resurrection narratives, the issue is not chronology but theology. What happened is more important than when it happened.

It is not uncommon to read or hear these stories read and think: "What I wouldn't give to have been there! Such momentous events would have certainly enlivened my faith; the exercise of such remarkable powers would have surely strengthened my resolve to serve others." In the second reading, Paul assures us that we did not have to be there to receive the power of the Spirit. We have all been baptized into the body of Christ. As members of that body, we proclaim that Jesus, not Caesar, or the king, or the president, or any other human power, is Lord. This is a real challenge in a world that holds up wealth and comfort, fame and power as idols to be worshiped. The Spirit has come to us, perhaps not through a mighty wind or the breath of the Risen Lord, but through the waters of baptism and the oils of anointing. Paul is speaking of all of us when he says: "To each individual the manifestation of the Spirit is given for some benefit." What might that be today?

Today's sequence lists some of the characteristics of the Spirit: "Father of the poor...comforter...blessed light...." These are the gifts of the Spirit that will renew the world—but they will only accomplish this through our agency. The manifestation of the Spirit is given to us so that we might work for justice for the poor, comfort those who mourn or who are in despair, bring light to those in darkness. Paul tells us: "There are different kinds of spiritual gifts...different forms of service...different workings." It is for each one of us to discover how the Spirit will work through us for the benefit of others. When we discover this and cooperate, there will be no limit to what the Spirit will be able to accomplish through us.

Praying with Scripture

- What natural gifts have you been given through which the Spirit can work?

- How have you used them in the past in the service of others? How might they be used now and in the future?

- Pray for the grace to forgive those who may have offended you.

Ordinary Time

FIRST SUNDAY IN ORDINARY TIME: BAPTISM OF THE LORD

SECOND SUNDAY IN ORDINARY TIME

Readings:
*Isa 62:1–5; Ps 96:1–3, 7–10;
1 Cor 12:4–11; John 2:1–11*

WE ARE INVITED TO A WEDDING

Everyone loves a wedding! It is a public manifestation of commitment to love, the beginning of a new family with all its promise, and a great time for a party. If it is such a time of happiness, why do people cry at weddings? Many people are simply overcome by emotion. But which emotion? Might it be that they realize that the couple has moved beyond their individual lives, as friends have known them, and is creating something new and extraordinary? They are basing the future of this new reality on trust in each other. To place one's future in the hands of another weak, limited human being is a remarkable act of trust, one that might well elicit strong emotion. Consequently, it was not by accident that Isaiah used the wedding metaphor to characterize the intimate bond between God and the people. Nor was it a coincidence that Jesus' first wondrous sign recorded in the Gospel of John occurred during a wedding feast. A wedding is a sign that love is strong enough to trust in another.

The imagery found in the first reading characterizes the love that God has for the people of Israel. Zion, the hill on which the city of Jerusalem was established, came to represent the city itself. Destroyed by the Babylonians, it is referred to by the prophet Isaiah as "Forsaken" and the land as "Desolate." But something new is about to take place. The city is about to be vindicated by the very God who had forsaken it. The covenant relationship is about to be reestablished and a new name given. Renaming always means a new status or a new creation. The people's name will be changed from "Forsaken" to "My Delight" and the land from "Desolate" to "Espoused." The wedding metaphor captures both excitement and hope. God is the one who initiates this new relationship; God is the one who will build up a new community. It seems that God's love is great enough that God will actually ground the future in trust in this weak human nation.

The very first sign that Jesus performs in the Gospel of John takes place at a wedding. The excitement and hope that surged through the wedding feast exemplify the excitement and hope that will mark his ministry. In this gospel, Jesus' miracles are called signs, meaning that they are outward manifestations of some deeper reality. To what reality does this sign point? Since a wedding signifies a new creation, this sign must somehow characterize something new. In the story, the water preserved in the stone jars is intended for Jewish ceremonial washing. Free flowing wine into which Jesus changed the water is a standard symbol of eschatological fulfillment. By performing this miracle, Jesus transforms a celebration of marital new life and hope into one of eschatological new life and hope.

Wedding celebrations also include gifts. In this new life of eschatological fulfillment, we have been given remarkable gifts. In the passage from 1 Corinthians, Paul lists a few of them: wisdom, knowledge, faith, healing, mighty deeds, prophecy, discernment of spirits, tongues and their interpretation. There are others as well: "love, joy, peace, patience, kindness, generosity, faithfulness, gentleness, self-control" (Gal 5:22). Weddings mean new life, a new creation. New Year's resolutions also suggest a new way of living, a kind of transformation. What would happen if we considered this New Year as the beginning of a new relationship with God, something like a wedding? How would the world change if each one of us took hold of even one of the marvelous gifts that we have been given by the Spirit and allowed it to transform our lives, like water transformed into good wine, and then shared it with others? Why can't such transformation be done? Isaiah recounted how the devastated Israel was restored; John reports how water became wine. The same Spirit, the same Lord, the same God works in us. Why can't it be done today?

Probably every one of us would rise to the occasion if we knew we had been chosen to make a difference, to launch a transformation. We would thrill to the idea of being chosen for any distinction. To think that we have what it takes to make a difference—now that is something! But we have been chosen. We are the ones who have been chosen to change the world. We are the ones called to bring about the peace for which so many people long. We have been given the responsibility to reform our world or our church. You may say: "We can't do it." Why not? Look at all of the marvelous gifts we have been given. Though God initiates the transformation, we can be part of changing what has been forsaken into a delight, what has been desolate into something that is espoused. We have been invited to the wedding of eschatological fulfillment. We have been chosen to make a difference.

Praying with Scripture

- Today is a good day to renew baptismal promises. What might they be calling you to do?

- What special gift have you received from God that you can share with others?

- Make a New Year's resolution that will make a difference.

THIRD SUNDAY IN ORDINARY TIME
Readings:
Neh 8:2–4a, 5–6, 8–10; Ps. 19:8–10, 15;
1 Cor 12:12–30; Luke 1:1–4; 4:14–21

THIS IS THE WORD OF THE LORD!

How can a message that was intended for people who lived thousands of years ago have any meaning for us today, when new generations can hardly endure the insights of their elders? Some of the stories in the Bible certainly make exciting action movies, but are we expected to live like that? To think as they did? To cherish the same aspirations? After all, the biblical stories came from an ancient preindustrial, pretechnological, eastern world. Isn't the newspaper more relevant to our lives than the Bible? These are valid questions. Some people answer them by walking away from the Bible. The readings for today provide a different response.

The first reading, taken from the little known biblical book Nehemiah, depicts a liturgical setting. Ezra the priest reads "plainly from the book of the law of God." He does not merely read the message; he interprets it so that all who hear can understand what is read. And who is his audience? "Men, women, and those children old enough to understand." The people have only recently returned to the land of Israel after having been exiled in Babylon for seventy years. While under foreign domination, they had not always been free to follow the precepts of their faith. Therefore, it was necessary to be instructed anew, to have the tradition reinterpreted for this new situation.

The people who hear Ezra weep when they realize the implications of what he is saying. The burden of their sinfulness and the sinfulness of their ancestors seems to be more than they can bear. But neither Ezra nor the Levites who assist him in the instruction of the people intend that they be overcome by their guilt. Instead they insist: "Today is holy…do not weep…rejoicing in the LORD must be your strength!" In other words, they are telling the people to learn from their mistakes, but to learn too that God is merciful.

A similar situation is depicted in the gospel passage. The author admits that he was not an eyewitness to the events that he is describing. Rather, he is handing down what had been handed down to him. The Greek word for *hand down* is a technical word for transmitting the tradition. This means that the entire gospel of Luke is a transmission of tradition about Jesus. The gospel reading itself depicts Jesus returning to the town where he grew up. As an adult man, he is invited to read from the scroll and to comment on the message of the passage. This he does, but the message he delivers is not what the other worshipers expect. The passage read is from the prophet Isaiah. At that time it was considered a portrait of the long-awaited Messiah. In his explanation, Jesus identifies himself as that individual. Those of us who know this gospel story are aware of how it ends. But the part of that story offered to us today does not tell us how ferociously the people of Nazareth responded. This omission is helpful to us, for now we can see ourselves in that assembly and we can decide how we will hear Jesus' interpretation.

These settings resemble our own liturgical assemblies, for it is there that we too hear the word of God and have it interpreted for us. Like the people who heard the instruction of Ezra and those to whom Jesus spoke, we are taught the meaning of God's word for our day. How do we hear it? Do we take it to heart? Or do we think its challenging message is intended for someone else? And those of us involved in biblical ministry, whether teaching or preaching, how do we break open that word for others? Do we simply tell them what the Bible says? Or do we bring its message into conversation with the contemporary world? Today's message from 1 Corinthians can be a test case.

In the second reading, Paul talks about diversity within the Christian community. He finds that the human body is a perfect metaphor for making his point. He argues that every part of the body is important for its proper functioning. Though each body part is different, each makes a necessary contribution to the body's overall well-being. Since the Corinthian community was struggling with the diversity of the spiritual gifts of its members, such as speaking in tongues or the powers of healing, Paul probably had this body metaphor in mind when he first chose the metaphor.

Though such spiritual diversity is seldom the cause of dissension today, contemporary believers are often challenged by other examples of difference. Parishes formerly made up of one ethnic group are now required to open themselves to other ethnic groups. Such changes are not always welcome. The same is true of our attitudes toward people in other parts of the world: those who are starving in Darfur, those who suffer from AIDS in Africa, those driven from their homes in the Middle East. Do we realize that they are as much a part of the body of Christ as we are? When we hear this, can we accept the fact that this too is the word of the Lord?

Praying with Scripture

- What might you do to deepen your understanding of the scriptures?

- Are you open to an interpretation of the Sunday readings that might be challenging?

- What gifts do you have that will contribute to the building up of the body of Christ?

FOURTH SUNDAY IN ORDINARY TIME
Readings:
Jer 1:4–5, 17–19; Ps 71:1–6, 15, 17;
1 Cor 12:31—13:13; Luke 4:21–30

I LOVE YOU; YOU'RE PERFECT; NOW CHANGE!

The title of today's reflection is the name of a highly acclaimed musical comedy that has made the rounds in some of the major cities of the country. It also describes some of the dynamics found in many human love relationships. It sometimes happens that we genuinely love someone and are captivated by that person's charm and wit, intelligence and sensitivity, unselfishness and caring disposition. But it is not uncommon that, despite our initial openness to the other, we soon feel a responsibility to overhaul what we think should be changed in that person. We claim that we want to make her or him better, to bring out the best that we know is there somewhere. On the musical stage, this attempt to improve another may be a sure recipe for wicked humor, but in real life it can undermine the love relationship and even tear it apart.

Some form of love underlies every memorable story ever told and most of the music that is composed. After all, we have all heard that "love makes the world go 'round." We know that love is a primary motivator of a good deal of human behavior, and that it also serves as a deterrent to unsavory ways of acting. When we are young, we think that we know so much about love, and we might even resent anyone telling us differently. Then, as we get older, we realize just how little we actually do know about it. Still, throughout life, everyone searches for some form of love, and for someone upon whom to lavish the love we have to offer.

Today's reading from 1 Corinthians is *the* classic definition of love. Even those people who do not cherish our biblical faith acknowledge this. While the reading might affirm the first part of the musical's title, namely, "I love you," it does not subscribe to the other two phrases. It does not demand that the loved one be perfect. In fact, if she or he were perfect, we would not have to be "patient," as Paul insists, nor would we have to "endure all things." And as for the last phrase of the title, the reading suggests that we ourselves, not those whom we love, are the ones who must now change. The musical comedy might be very entertaining, but this biblical exhortation calls us to a kind of self-emptying that is close to heroic.

As we read the list of love's characteristics, we realize just how countercultural love is. Our society does not encourage us to be patient or even kind. In fact, it admonishes us to seek our own interests, to look out for Number One. It applauds pomposity and ego-inflation by making icons of movie stars, sports heroes, and musical performers. And we become complicit in this empty adulation when we unthinkingly pay tribute to them at their various altars. Furthermore, so much within the media promotes rudeness and quick tempers. And as far as truth is concerned, this is not always a valued commodity. In fact, we may feel that we have been lied to so many times that we are suspicious of anyone who claims to be telling the truth.

The gospel reading tells us that the people of Nazareth were fickle in their acceptance of Jesus. At first "all spoke highly of him and were amazed at the gracious words that came from his mouth," but they soon turned against him. Theirs was not the kind of love described by Paul. They spoke highly of Jesus, because they wanted him to perform for them the kind of miracles he had performed in Capernaum. They wanted a messiah who would work miracles, not one who would challenge them to live differently, to love unselfishly and wholeheartedly. Jesus, on the other hand, was more like the prophet described in the reading from the Book of Jeremiah. There we find one who was told to gird his loins, something done when preparing for a strenuous activity like battle. He had to be ready to face those who "will fight against you." The prophet faced such opposition, and Jesus did as well, for the people of his own town rose up against him and sought to hurl him off a cliff.

Despite the fact that we all want and need love, it seems to be so difficult to give it. If we stop for a moment and reflect, however, we might discover that we can indeed point to such love in our lives. The people we really admire the most are those who are indeed patient and kind, not jealous or pompous, not inflated or rude, not quick-tempered or brooding. They are people who genuinely love, people after whom we might want to model ourselves rather than make over. They are people who are not misled by flattery or crushed by opposition. They are genuine people who have discovered what love really means, what Paul calls the "more excellent way."

Praying with Scripture

- Read the passage from Corinthians slowly and prayerfully. Which aspect of love do you find most challenging?

- Do you love people for who they are or for what they might do for you?

- How do you deal with opposition? With defensiveness or resentment? Or with genuine love?

FIFTH SUNDAY IN ORDINARY TIME
Readings:
Isa 6:1–2a, 3–8; Ps 138:1–5, 7–8;
1 Cor 15:1–11; Luke 5:1–11

HAND-ME-DOWNS

It is not unlikely that, while we were growing up, we wore clothing or played with toys that had been handed down to us from an older sibling or cousin. At such times, we grew into the clothing or took possession of the toys, making them our own. Now, as independent as we adults might like to think we are, in many ways we are still dependent on what has been handed down to us. This includes such basic realities as our cultural identity, our language and history, many of our values, and, certainly, our religious tradition.

In the Letter to the Corinthians, Paul speaks of such "handing down." He handed down to his Christian converts what he had received, so that they, in their turn, might hand it down to others—and so on and so on, until the religious tradition, which has been preserved yet reshaped in this process of transmission, is handed down to us. Now that we have received it, it is both our privilege and our responsibility to take our place in this ongoing process of transmission and to hand down the tradition to yet another generation.

What kind of people are called to transmit the religious tradition? Saints? Scholars? Someone other than me? The people called by God in today's readings clearly and honestly identify themselves as unlikely transmitters of the tradition. Isaiah was "a man of unclean lips" (Isa 6:5); Paul called himself "the least of the apostles," because he "persecuted the church of God" (1 Cor 15:9); Peter admitted that he was "a sinful man" (Luke 5:8). We see from this that the treasure, which is our religious tradition, is entrusted to weak, limited, sinful people like you and me—the only kind of people there are.

The call to participate in transmitting the religious tradition comes to ordinary people within the normal circumstances of their everyday lives. Isaiah was in the Temple, which was not an unusual place to find an observant Israelite. The apostles, who were Galilean fishermen, were plying their trade on Lake Gennesaret. People are inspired in places and through events that are usually quite ordinary. What is remarkable is not what they are doing, but what they experience at these places and in these events. Isaiah was transformed so that he could proclaim God's word; the apostles were granted the courage they needed to bring others into their company.

For many of us, our call to participate in this ongoing process will probably be far less dramatic than was the call of Isaiah. Still, we may well have responded as generously as he did, even though we may not have realized it. In our own way, we have declared: "Here I am; send me!"—to teach or preach, to write or publish the good news. Send me to shape the minds and hearts of our children in the values that I have received. Send me to express God's beauty through music, art, or poetry, to demonstrate God's justice through the way I conduct business, to impart God's compassion toward those in desperate need of comfort. Send me to announce to the world, by the way I live my life, that the tradition has been handed down and is indeed alive in me.

We should not expect to see dramatic signs, such as the miraculous catch of fish witnessed by the apostles. We who prefer immediate results may not enjoy the fruits of our labors. But, then, there is probably a good deal of embellishment in the gospel story, embellishment that was meant to point out to those who heard it the extraordinary dimension present in ordinary reality. Without such embellishment we might otherwise overlook the action of God in the event on the lake, as we do so often in our own lives.

As stated earlier, when the tradition is handed down, its essence is preserved yet reshaped. In other words, its dynamic message keeps addressing the needs of the current time, not those of the past. Because these needs change, the message is sometimes reshaped. For example, Paul reminded the Corinthians that the gospel that he preached saved them. But saved them from what? Corinth was renowned for its unbridled sexual behavior. An ancient seaport, it was also an important commercial center. People there probably offered homage to fertility gods as well as to deities that promised prosperity. People today may not offer sacrifice to statues, but sexual license and inordinate consumerism certainly still plague us. In handing down the tradition, Paul's summons to righteous living must be reshaped so that people today can hear and understand its challenge as if it were being spoken directly to them—for it is. Today we stand with Isaiah in the Temple, or with the apostles on the shore of the sea, or with Paul in the midst of a thriving metropolis. We are the heirs of the tradition, a tradition that must be handed down if it is to remain alive and entrusted to the next generation.

Praying with Scripture

- Pray the psalm response, being particularly grateful to God for those who have handed down the tradition to you.

- In what ways do you already hand down aspects of the tradition? How might you do this better?

- How do you deepen your knowledge of our religious tradition?

SIXTH SUNDAY IN ORDINARY TIME

Readings:
Jer 17:5–8; Ps 1:1–4, 6;
1 Cor 15:12, 16–20; Luke 6:17, 20–26

BLESSINGS AND CURSES

What comes to mind when you think of blessings? Perhaps some degree of prosperity or good health. Our musings might include something as weighty as deliverance from harm, or as commonplace as victory in a high-school basketball game. When circumstances seem to go the way we want, it is not uncommon for us to consider this a blessing.

And what about curses? We don't have to turn to witches' spells in fairy tales to find them. Cursing language is quite common in everyday speech. Even children cry out: "Drop dead!" or "Go to h———!" They probably don't realize it, but these are genuine curses. We may not believe that we have been cursed when misfortune befalls us, but we certainly do think that we have somehow been handed a "raw deal" and that someone other than ourselves is responsible for our bad luck.

People in traditional societies, like those that produced the Bible, believed that certain styles of speech possessed extraordinary power. They were convinced that when one pronounced the words of blessing or curse the words themselves began the process of bringing about the objective. Therefore, they did not throw out words of blessing or curse randomly, as we might today. They further realized that if human words could accomplish such feats, one could only imagine what God's words might be able to do.

Both the reading from Jeremiah and the gospel passage speak of blessings and curses (woes). Though the terms are not used in exactly the same way in both readings, they do give us an insight into the kind of behavior that was to be preferred, and they sketch some of the consequences of that behavior in human life. Both

Jeremiah and the psalmist use striking nature imagery to contrast the life circumstances of those who trust in God or cherish God's law with those who do not. The righteous will thrive even in hard times and will be a source of life for others. On the other hand, the wicked will have barely enough life force to live and will lack any power of fertility.

The contrast drawn by Jeremiah is not difficult to comprehend. It promotes common religious sentiments, namely, trust in God and respect for God's law. When we turn to the gospel, we discover that its message is quite revolutionary. Jesus seems to turn reality upside down. Those whom Jesus calls blessed live lives that we would normally consider cursed; and those threatened with woes are enjoying blessings. What does this mean? Does God really prefer the poor and needy and reject those with financial security? There are clues in this gospel reading that show us that this is not really the case. What makes one blessed is not simply poverty or hunger or sadness, but commitment to the Son of Man (v22), and, like the false prophets of old, the ones condemned are those who compromised their values in order to be accepted and succeed. This closer look shows us that Jesus' message is actually very similar to Jeremiah's and the one found in the psalm response: Trust God and cherish God's law. In other words, if you choose God, you will be blessed. Conversely, if you choose human standards, you will succumb to the consequences of woe.

We today have a very narrow understanding of law, especially the law of God. We think of it as being rigid and confining; we may even consider it out of date and irrelevant. Ancient Israel believed that the law set a path or direction to happiness and fulfillment. They saw it as "refreshing the soul...rejoicing the heart" (Ps 19:8–10). Cherishing God's law was not a burden for them; it was a blessing.

Still, trust in God is easier said than done, because we are all so influenced by the standards of the day. We are bombarded by ads that assure us that we have a right to a high paying job, even without working for it; the exceptionally wealthy are held up to us as icons to be emulated, and the needy are disdained as unworthy of our attention. At every turn we are offered food—"all you can eat," and the only valid reason for depriving oneself of it is the desire to lose weight in order to achieve "the body beautiful."

The weeping of which Jesus speaks is probably the frustration that people on the margins experience when they are denied the opportunities that every society owes all its citizens, not merely those who have status and privilege.

These Beatitudes challenge our understanding of blessedness, but they also are sometimes difficult to interpret. Surely Jesus is not suggesting that those who are poor or hungry or grieving should be satisfied with their lot in life because they will eventually experience a reversal of fortune. Rather, he is saying that the values and customs of the reign of God are at times in serious conflict with those of society. Today's readings urge us to step back from the hustle and bustle of life and evaluate our values from Jesus' point of view.

Praying with Scripture

- Consider the real blessings of your life, and thank God for them.
- In what ways do the blessings or Beatitudes of the gospel challenge the standards by which you live?
- How can you serve as an agent through whom God blesses the people society has overlooked?

SEVENTH SUNDAY IN ORDINARY TIME
Readings:
1 Sam 26:2, 7–9, 12–13, 22–23; Ps 103:1–4, 8, 10, 12–13; 1 Cor 15:45–49; Luke 6:27–38

THE GOLDEN RULE

As children we learned the golden rule: "Do unto others as you would have them do unto you." Then as we grew older, we realized that the world operates according to a significantly different version of that rule: "Do unto others before they can do unto you!" We were told: "Don't give an inch! Hit 'em where it hurts!" Many of us have become convinced that the only way to get ahead is to get there first and to grab what we can. We think that the only way to survive is to assume an offensive stance and hit before we are hit. Unfortunately, in many cases, this appears to be all too true.

It is hard enough to follow this ancient rule when we are in charge of the situation, but how are we expected to act when we are in vulnerable circumstances? Are we required to do good to those who have perpetrated evil upon us? The answer is "yes!" An example of this is found in the passage from 1 Samuel. There we read that King Saul was threatened by David's popularity, so the king gathered a vast army and set out to kill him. When David came upon a sleeping Saul, he could have driven a spear through the vulnerable king and thereby delivered himself from Saul's jealousy once and for all. Instead, acknowledging that Saul was God's chosen king, David left evidence that he had been there so that Saul might realize that he had spared his life. This is a striking example of respect and forgiveness, of doing unto others what you would have them do unto you.

The golden rule does not require that we allow others to take advantage of us. The gospel makes that very clear. There we read that Jesus is teaching his disciples that they must love those who mistreat them. How is this to be done? He provides a few examples. First, the one who was struck on the cheek, whether as an attack or as an insult, is told to rise above it and to show who is really in charge of the situation. Second, the one who is forced to give up a cloak was directed to act in like manner and to relinquish even the tunic. In both instances, the individuals who suffer some form of abuse refuse to be victims or to retaliate. By their actions they say: "I can outdo your violence toward me with my willingness to give freely much more than you sought to take from me. Therefore, I am really in charge." In this way they stand with David in his attitude toward Saul. They overcome evil with good.

Is it really possible to forgive our enemies in a world torn by wars of all kinds, economic disparity, and the exploitation of the vulnerable? Can we do good to those who terrorize us, who torture and kill those we love? Can we even forgive them? We are not expected to overlook these evils, but "we shall...bear the image of the heavenly one" and, therefore, we are called to forgive them and not retaliate. We are called to be merciful and not vengeful. To act in such a way is true heroism, and, as followers of Christ, we are called to it. It has been said that genuine love of real enemies is the most distinguishing characteristic of the Christian.

In the second reading we find Paul, with his unique theological approach, contrasting Adam, who was formed from the earth, with Christ, who came down from heaven. He states that the first man was "a living being"; the second one is a "life-giving spirit." As always, the real concern of Paul's teaching is genuine Christian behavior. He argues here that, though we were born in the image of the first man (Adam), by baptism we bear the image of the second man (Christ). In other words, while we may be tempted to live according to society's version of the rule ("Do unto others before they can do unto you"), we are called to live the gospel's version, which challenges us to love our enemies as we love ourselves.

There are too many examples of violence, hatred, and revenge in our world to list here; yet there are also examples of amazing forgiveness and genuine love. Countries such as South Africa and Bosnia have instituted "truth and reconciliation" courts, where people who have inflicted unspeakable atrocities on others are forgiven by some of the very ones who were their victims. We have also heard of bereaved individuals who have shown mercy to those who murdered their loved ones. Such people are present-day replicas of the crucified Jesus who, in the throes of bitter agony, cried out: "Father, forgive them" (Luke 23:34).

Most of us will probably not be called upon to demonstrate such extraordinary love, but we can all show kindness to others, even to those whom we do not particularly like or who do not care for us. After all, violence and hatred will be eradicated from this world only if we refuse to perpetuate it.

Praying with Scripture

- Who in your life really needs your forgiveness? Can you give it?

- Pray for the grace to be able to forgive those who are considered our national enemies.

- Sometime this week perform "a random act of kindness."

EIGHTH SUNDAY IN ORDINARY TIME
Readings:
Sir 27:4–7; Ps 92:2–3, 13–16;
1 Cor 15:54–58; Luke 6:39–45

APPEARANCES CAN BE DECEIVING

We have all heard it said: "You have only one chance to make a good impression." Consequently, people often take great pains to make a good first impression. They choose clothing that will enhance their appearance; they demonstrate graciousness and charm; they choose their words carefully; and they smile and laugh at the appropriate times. There may be nothing wrong with such behavior, but it is not always genuine.

We cannot deny that in so many ways our society is obsessed with external appearances. We almost idolize the youthful body form, the face devoid of wrinkles, and the "six-pack" sculptured abs. We seem to be mesmerized by designer clothing and eye-popping jewelry. If we are honest with ourselves, we will have to admit that this aspect of our culture has left its mark on many of us. We ourselves may not possess many of these items, but we certainly wish that we did.

On the other hand, we also know that appearances can be deceiving. Clothing does not make the person; graciousness and charm can be superficial, and pleasing speech can be studied. As we gain wisdom, we put aside our preoccupation with externals and seek the deeper meaning of life. We realize that what is important is not what one appears to be, but who one really is. We have to admit that youthful appearance and the beauty associated

with it are truly only skin deep, and then we become more interested in character. We recognize that we are genuine only when
our words and actions correspond with our deepest aspirations
and convictions.

Today's reading from Sirach and the selection from the
Gospel of Luke focus on this human characteristic. Since interest
in human behavior is the primary concern of the Wisdom tradition, these passages employ wisdom forms of instruction, namely,
the proverb and the parable. The settings in which this instruction is found are quite commonplace, agriculture and social inter-
action, demonstrating that the lessons of life are learned in
everyday occurrences.

The reading from Sirach contains wisdom that has been
gleaned from life experience. The sage actually warns against first
impressions. He counsels his hearers to attend to a person's
speech, not to their outward guise. Using nature imagery, he compares that guise to a husk that hides from view the real source of
energy. It is speech that breaks open such husks and reveals what
is deep within. In another metaphor he compares speech with the
fruit of a tree. Just as the quality of that fruit is evidence of the
care taken of the tree, so one's speech reveals what is in one's
mind and heart. It is true that a person can cultivate a pleasing
manner of communication. But if such speech is not genuine, in
some unguarded moment the person's true character will eventually be revealed. Finally, Sirach maintains that one's moral fiber is
tested not in the acclamation of the crowd but in one's experience
of tribulation. Here he appeals to the experience of the potter. The
pot is only useful if it can pass the test of the oven. Otherwise it
has no strength or durability, and no usefulness.

The gospel depicts Jesus as a wisdom teacher, employing the
wisdom forms to make his points. Like Sirach before him, Jesus
appeals to nature. Good trees produce good fruit; bad trees produce bad fruit. So it is with people. Good people bring forth what
is good; evil people act in ways that are evil. The reading ends
with an adage that might have been found in Sirach: "From the
fullness of the heart the mouth speaks."

Jesus has no time for hypocrites, those who claim to have
morals or virtues but who do not possess or practice them. The
word *hypocrite* comes from the Greek for play-acting or pretense,

which is precisely what the hypocrite is engaged in. Jesus is particularly disturbed by hypocritical self-righteousness, and he castigates those who find fault with others while neglecting to correct their own faults. Such behavior gives the impression that they are faultless. Jesus insists that they not only have faults, but their hypocritical self-righteousness prevents them from recognizing them. Hypocrites cannot recognize the difference between the splinter in another's eye and a beam in their own eye. Once again, appearances are deceiving.

In the passage from 1 Corinthians, Paul takes the metaphor of clothing in an entirely different direction. He argues that in a certain context, clothing does indeed make the person. The clothing of which he speaks is the garb of incorruptibility, the attire of immortality. This clothing provides incorruptibility for those who are corruptible, immortality for those who are mortal. How is this possible? Because Christ has been victorious over death, and God grants us this same victory through our union with Christ. There is no self-righteousness here, no hypocrisy, no playacting or pretense. There is no need to strip us of any facade, for the exalted state to which we will be raised is genuine. We will truly be what we appear to be.

Praying with Scripture

- Reflect on your speech. What does it tell you about yourself? Are you kind and understanding, or are you judgmental?

- Which good works reveal your deepest aspirations and convictions?

- Pray for the grace to follow Paul's injunction: "Be firm, steadfast, always fully devoted to the work of the Lord."

NINTH SUNDAY IN ORDINARY TIME
Readings:
1 Kgs 8:41–43; Ps 117:1–2;
Gal 1:1–2, 6–10; Luke 7:1–10

WHO REALLY BELONGS?

We all want to belong to something. We are born into a family that provides us with racial, ethnic, national, and religious identity. We live in neighborhoods, though we can decide to what extent we desire to participate in them. We join parish communities and clubs. All of this indicates that, regardless of how independent we like to think we are, we are still fundamentally social beings. Belonging to these groups draws lines of differentiation, lines that identify the insiders and the outsiders. There is nothing wrong with this differentiation; in fact, it is quite normal. There are times, however, when differentiation can deteriorate into discrimination. When this happens, we have a problem.

We live in a world that is rife with various forms of discrimination. For years Catholics and Protestants fought a bloody war in Ireland; the long-standing racial apartheid structures of South Africa have only recently been abolished; the conflict in Rwanda was the result of tribal warfare, as are the struggles in Sudan, Nigeria, and Indonesia, to name but a few situations. At the breakup of the Soviet Union, Yugoslavia, and Iraq, festering ethnic rivalries previously held in check by the strong hand of a powerful leader flashed to the surface when that leader was deposed. Though many countries have outlawed overt discrimination, it still finds a comfortable home in the minds and hearts of many people, and this country is not exempt from such bias. All of this shows that we are in need of reform and transformation.

Many people hold that ancient Israel was ethnocentric, and it certainly was. After all, it did claim to be God's chosen people; it believed that it had a God-given right to the land of Canaan; it considered its religion superior to all other ancient religions; it maintained that its people were pure while other people were defiled. Without justifying such presumption, it is important that we understand why they might think these ways They were, after all, a minor nation in the ancient Near Eastern world; they were backward when compared to other cultures; for most of their existence they lived under the control of first the Egyptians, then the Babylonians, the Assyrians, and the Greeks. This is not to say that they were wrong in their perception of their importance. Rather, it is not uncommon for vulnerable people to perceive their survival as evidence of divine providence. The ancient Israelites may have been ethnocentric, but they did not believe their blessings were meant for them alone. The first reading for today is evidence of this.

The Temple of Solomon was remarkable. Standing three stories high, its walls were paneled with cedar; figures decorating the walls were inlaid with gold; doorposts were made of olivewood, and the floor and doors came from wood of the fir tree; Temple vessels were fashioned from bronze and gold. Today's first reading is taken from Solomon's prayer at the dedication of this marvelous Temple. In it, he prays for the foreigner. This was not the resident alien who settled in the land and was protected by Israelite law. Solomon prays for the stranger from a distant land, one who heard of God's great name and came to honor God. Though he prays that such an "outsider" might come to know and fear God, he asks that God will "do all that foreigner asks of you." This last part of his prayer shows that Solomon respected foreigners as they were, not as they might become if they conformed to the pattern set by the Israelites.

The gospel reading shows that Jesus too respected the foreigner. Actually, the centurion whose slave Jesus healed was more than a foreigner; he was a member of the occupying Roman army. One could say that he was the enemy. Yet, when he sent emissaries to Jesus, asking that he come and heal the man's slave, Jesus went immediately with them. The strict Jewish laws of purity forbade Jesus to associate with this foreigner, but Jesus was not deterred. He went wherever there was need. Later in the story we find Jesus praising the centurion for his faith, but the faith of the man is not mentioned at the outset.

So much hatred and violence are perpetrated in today's world in the name of racial purity, ethnic loyalty, national patriotism, and religious orthodoxy. We would do well to take to heart the message of these readings. Both Solomon and Jesus were open and accepting of the men who came to them. They did not question their integrity, nor did they demand that the men renounce their loyalties and comply with norms not their own. Neither Solomon nor Jesus thought that these men did not belong. In the very midst of the Temple, the place considered by Israelites as the holiest place in the world, Solomon recognized the integrity of the religious seeker, and he gathered that person's prayer into his own. Jesus was willing to go to the home of a foreigner in order to bring him and his slave into the embrace of God's healing circle. Can we do less?

Praying with Scripture

- What can you do to make "outsiders" feel that they belong?

- Include people of other religious faiths and traditions in your prayers.

- Open yourself to those in need regardless of their racial, ethnic, national, or religious identity.

TENTH SUNDAY IN ORDINARY TIME
Readings:
1 Kgs 17:17–24; Ps 30:2, 4–6, 11–13; Gal 1:11–19; Luke 7:11–17

SOCIETY'S MOST VULNERABLE

Who are the most vulnerable in our society? There are far too many people who might merit that designation. There are always the obvious groups: the helpless children who are exploited by the very ones who should protect them; the desperately poor who must choose between heat and food; the homeless who carry their belongings with them in plastic bags wherever they go; the chronically ill who have neither financial means nor insurance; the elderly who lose not only their physical and mental powers but also their human dignity. There are others who come to mind as well: the mentally ill who wander through the streets of our cities with no one to care for them or support them; the immigrants who suffer discrimination because of the color of their skin, the shape of the eyes, their ethnic identity, or their religious allegiance; the needy who are bogged down by government agencies that seem to be working against them; the military personnel who return from an unpopular war with serious interior wounds that cannot be seen and, therefore, are never treated. For a society that prides itself on its accomplishments, we have not attended well to those among us who are most vulnerable.

It cannot be denied that, like all other ancient cultures, Israel was sometimes quite violent toward other nations as well as toward its own people. Still, as a communal-oriented society, it had laws that protected its own citizens and the aliens who lived within its borders. The normal way this was accomplished was through its patriarchal structures. The men were responsible for all the members of their households. This included slaves and guests. Some people undoubtedly slipped through the cracks, however. The major groups in that category were the widows who did not have husband, son, or brother to protect them, the orphans who were also bereft of patriarchal guardianship, and the resident aliens who enjoyed no legal status. A prescription in Israel's law, however, looked out for those vulnerable ones in ways that the patriarchal structure did not (Deut 14:29; 26:12–13).

Today's first reading tells of a woman, a resident of Zarephath in Sidon, a territory outside of the confines of the land of Israel, who was doubly disadvantaged. Besides being a woman who had no legal status in the community, she was a widow with no male guardian. Furthermore, her son, her only hope for future advocacy, was on the point of death. Surely this woman was one of the most vulnerable members of society. Still, it was to her that the prophet Elijah went seeking hospitality, and she did not disappoint him. When her son fell ill she thought that the prophet was somehow responsible for this misfortune. Despite this, she entrusted her son, who had stopped breathing, to Elijah. Her hospitality and trust were rewarded, for Elijah was able to revive the boy. Because of this marvel, the woman was able to recognize Elijah as a man of God.

A similar story is found in the reading from the gospel. There we see Jesus encounter a widow who was taking her only son to his grave. Her situation was probably as dire as was the situation of the woman from Zarephath. The compassion that Jesus showed her was unexpected. He simply came upon the burial procession as it was leaving the city and he was approaching it. It is easy to think that Jesus was moved with pity for her because of the death of her child, but neither can the dire circumstances of her status in patriarchal society be denied. She was not merely a grieving mother; she was also one of the most vulnerable members of society. Because of the marvel she witnessed, the woman was able to recognize Jesus as a prophet of God.

These two stories clearly show that God does indeed choose the weak ones of the world to confound the strong. This should not have surprised the Israelites, for they saw themselves as the vulnerable ones in the ancient world. Nor should it surprise us. Those who are vulnerable know from experience that they cannot always depend upon others. There is no guarantee that they will then turn to God, but frequently there is no other place to turn. We must be careful that we do not romanticize these vulnerable individuals. The women did not earn the favors they received. They received them simply because they were vulnerable. It was only afterward that they praised God. The same is true today. We must be concerned about the vulnerable because they are vulnerable, not because they are deserving. It may happen that they will not even thank us for the help or protection we might give. That makes no difference.

We might ask how God will protect and care for the vulnerable, for those who seem to fall through the cracks. The answer is simple: God cares for them through us. We are the ones today who, in various and sundry ways, protect those who are without protection, who give hope to those who feel hopeless, who show the vulnerable that they are not outside of our circle of care.

Praying with Scripture

- Who are some of the vulnerable people in your society? What might you do to help them either individually or through the political process?

- How open are you to receive people who are not part of your circle?

- Pray for the grace to realize that, even in your own most vulnerable moments, God has not forsaken you.

ELEVENTH SUNDAY IN ORDINARY TIME
Readings:
2 Sam 12:7–10, 13; Ps 32:1–2, 5, 7, 11; Gal 2:16, 19–21; Luke 7:36—8:3

FORGIVE US OUR TRESPASSES

As perhaps the best-known prayer in the world, the Our Father is a remarkable testimony to our faith. Despite its gender-specific language that troubles so many, it is prayed by hundreds of millions of people every day. In it we acknowledge our family relationship with God, God's universal supremacy, and our total dependence on divine providence. We pray that God's plan of salvation be accomplished in and through us, and that we will be able to withstand the temptations that assail us. While some of the needs mentioned in the prayer may not immediately touch every life at all times, the prayer contains one petition that does: "Forgive us our trespasses." Whether or not we have updated the language to say "sins," the meaning is the same. We are all sinners, and we all need God's forgiveness.

We probably know the prayer so well, or we recite it so often, that its religious significance no longer makes an impression on us. After all, though we all might be able to admit that we are sinners, we are annoyed if anyone points out specific examples of our weakness. Besides, most of us have probably never been guilty of the kind of sins described in today's readings. This may be true, not because we are such good people, but because we have not been in situations that call forth the worst in us. If we look carefully at these readings, however, we might find that we share many of the same attitudes found in the sinners depicted there.

In the first reading, we find that David's weaknesses have caught up with him. Earlier he had been overcome with lust for the wife of another man. He certainly was not the first person, nor would he be the last, who became infatuated with someone with prior commitments. Unfortunately, he succumbed to the temptation, as has been the case with so many people before and after him. The attraction was not the sin; acting on it was. As frequently happens, the consequences of his behavior could not be avoided; Bathsheba conceived a child. Now what was he to do? How could he cover up his transgression? Again, in this he is not unlike many of us. As king, however, David had opportunities to hide what he had done. He tried to manipulate the situation and make it appear that the child belonged to Bathsheba's rightful husband, Uriah. But this was to no avail, for Uriah's basic integrity prevented him from enjoying the comfort of marital relations while the soldiers under his command were fighting. So David resorted to the vilest plan—he saw to it that Uriah died in battle. This left Bathsheba free to be taken into the royal household. This is a sorry picture of lust, fear, dishonesty, abuse of power, and ultimately murder. We may not have killed another person, but who has not been guilty of one or more of the other offenses?

Once David's sins had been uncovered, he did not try to deny his guilt or place the blame elsewhere. He acknowledged his culpability and cried out: "I have sinned against the LORD." Speaking in God's name, the prophet Nathan assured David that he had been forgiven. It should be noted that the one who gave this assurance is the very one who pointed out David's list of sins. Though the king had the power to silence the accusing prophet, he listened humbly to Nathan's words, accepted responsibility for his own actions, and acknowledged his sinfulness. David is an example of the repentant sinner.

The gospel passage recounts an episode that took place in the home of a highly reputed interpreter of the Law. Being a Pharisee, Simon, in whose home a dinner was held, would have known that contact with a public sinner placed Jesus in jeopardy of becoming ritually unclean. Jesus never denied the woman's sinfulness; instead, he pointed out the correspondence between a sinner's need of forgiveness and the depth of grateful love inspired by receiving that forgiveness. For his part, Simon not only condemned the woman, but he also passed judgment on Jesus for allowing her to touch him. In his self-righteous estimation of his own propriety, Simon overlooked the fact that he failed to fulfill the requirements of hospitality, a very serious obligation in the ancient Near Eastern culture.

True, the woman's need of forgiveness was much greater than was Simon's, but that was precisely Jesus' point. If there was a correspondence between the need of forgiveness and the resulting grateful love, as Jesus argued earlier, then her love far excelled Simon's. Their respective behavior demonstrated the truth of this. Simon showed no compunction for having violated the protocol of hospitality. She, on the other hand, fulfilled that protocol with exaggerated solemnity, bathing Jesus' feet with her tears, wiping them with her hair, kissing his feet, and anointing them with oil. Her sins may have been great, but so were her contrition and the love from which it sprang. What can be said of our sorrow for sin?

Praying with Scripture

- Do you take responsibility for your moral failures, or do you try to cover them up and make excuses for yourself?

- Are you quick to judge others and pride yourself for your apparent righteousness, or are you grateful for God's mercy toward you?

- Pray the act of contrition slowly and reflectively.

TWELFTH SUNDAY IN ORDINARY TIME
Readings:
Zech 12:10–11; 13:1; Ps 63:2–6, 8–9;
Gal 3:26–29; Luke 9:18–24

WHO WAS HE? WHO ARE WE?

Human identity is very complicated. We receive it, yet we must shape it; we are told what it is, yet we must discover it. Names are a part of this identity. Some names like "Junior" indicate one's relationship with another; others, like "Angelina," reflect who was popular at the time of one's birth. We are often named after family members as a sign of honor, or after saints in hope that we might model our lives after them. We have formal names known to most others, personal names known to some, and nicknames known to our intimate friends. If we don't like our names, we sometimes change them. But names help to identify who we are.

The gospel story is about Jesus' identity. It does not address any of his personal or family characteristics. Outside of the Christmas stories, very few biblical passages are concerned with these aspects of Jesus. In the reading from Luke's gospel, Jesus inquires about the people's perception of him as a religious figure: "Who do the crowds say that I am?" The answers given are telling. They probably indicate the kind of figure they hoped Jesus would be rather than the kind of person they actually perceived in him. The figure of John the Baptist is an example of this. There seems to have been a striking difference between Jesus and John. All of the gospels indicate this. John left the inhabited regions of the land and retreated into the wilderness of Judea, while Jesus made the villages the center of his activity. John lived a very ascetic life, feeding on a diet of honey and locusts, while Jesus and his disciples were often guests at banquets. John himself contrasted his own baptism of repentance with Jesus' baptism of the Spirit.

So, identifying Jesus with John may have been more wishful thinking than actual recognition.

Why would anyone think that Jesus was John? Or Elijah? Or one of the ancient prophets, for that matter? Because these men were considered forerunners of the Messiah. Thus, if the people could cast Jesus in the guise of one of these men, then perhaps he was indeed that long-awaited figure. And was he any of these men? When Jesus asked Peter: "But who do you say that I am?" the disciple declared: "The Christ of God." In other words, he was not a forerunner returned from the dead. He was the Messiah (the Hebrew word for "anointed" as Christ is the Greek word). Jesus does not correct Peter, but he identifies himself with another ancient title, which suggests the kind of Messiah he will be. That title, Son of Man, calls to mind the mysterious figure found in the pages of the Book of Daniel (Dan 7:13). Jesus is from God, and he was given by God dominion over the heavens and the earth; however, Jesus radically alters the character of this figure: "The Son of Man must suffer greatly."

Jesus did not live into any of the names others gave him. Instead, he reinterpreted the meaning associated with those names. He was indeed the Messiah, not simply a remarkable human religious figure as were John, Elijah, or the prophets. He was indeed a heavenly figure, but not one robed in splendor and glory, at least not until he would rise from the dead. It is no wonder the people of his time did not understand him—but then, do we?

The theme of suffering is also found in today's passage from the prophet Zechariah. This oracle of lamentation mentions the Day of the Lord, a period of suffering that will precede the time of eschatological fulfillment. Pairing this reading with the gospel passage focuses our attention on a single individual, one who has suffered at the hands of others, rather than on the people as a whole. In this way, the innocent suffering of Jesus is reinforced. Returning to the gospel, we see that it is not only Christ who will suffer, but also those who wish to follow him. This raises a second question: Who are we?

Paul sketches our profile in the selection from the Letter to the Galatians. We are Abraham's descendants; we are children of God; we are one in Christ. As descendants of Abraham, we inherit all of the promises made to that great patriarch. The best-known promises include land and children—in other words, security and a future. Another important though lesser-known promise stated: "All the communities of the earth shall find blessing in you" (Gen 12:3). This means that we will be a source of blessing for others. As children of God we share in the very life of God, and we enjoy all of the blessings that flow from that honor. Being one in Christ means that our very real ethnic, social, or gender differences do not create hierarchies of privilege. We are all privileged. But the final word remains; we will have to pay a price for this privilege. We must be willing to take up our cross and follow our Messiah.

Praying with Scripture

- Which of Jesus' titles most appeals to you? Why? What might this tell you about yourself?

- Which of the references used by Paul best identifies your sense of yourself as a Christian?

- Which difficulties in your life offer you an opportunity to take up your cross and follow Jesus?

THIRTEENTH SUNDAY IN ORDINARY TIME
Readings:
1 Kgs 19:16b, 19–21; Ps 16:1–2, 5, 7–11; Gal 5:1, 13–18; Luke 9:51–62

THE COST OF DISCIPLESHIP

The great Lutheran theologian Dietrich Bonhoeffer wrote a series of reflections on the Sermon on the Mount entitled *The Cost of Discipleship*. In them he maintained that discipleship requires that we make a fundamental decision to follow Jesus and accept the consequences of that decision. The ultimate cost of discipleship was exacted of Bonhoeffer himself when, on April 9, 1945, he was hanged by the Nazis for his participation in the German Resistance and his involvement in attempts to assassinate Hitler. While discipleship might force some people to decide between life and death, few of us will be asked to pay that ultimate price. Genuine discipleship does, however, call us to live in a way that, at times, may require a certain degree of heroism.

The readings for today demonstrate this cost of discipleship. Elisha was required to leave his parents if he wished to be a disciple of the great prophet Elijah. Since kinship was probably the strongest tie in the ancient Near Eastern world, to leave one's family involved more than emotional detachment. Some saw it as turning away from one's most basic responsibilities, as well as from the support and protection that this fundamental bond guaranteed. Only with grave reason did one set them aside. Elisha was not forced to follow Elijah. In fact, the prophet responded to Elisha's hesitation: "Go back! Have I done anything to you?" Once Elisha made his decision, however, he not only left his home, but he also destroyed the tools of his former occupation. In this way he indicated that the break with his former life was complete and there was no turning back.

The people who wished to follow Jesus were also told that they must leave behind all family responsibilities and privileges. Furthermore, they would have to learn to live without the security of a stable home. Finally, like Elisha before them, this commitment would have to be complete. No looking back. If we read the gospels carefully, we find that only some of the very closest disciples of Jesus were asked to leave all and follow Jesus, yet this story seems to imply that everyone was expected to make that kind of sacrifice. Is there a contradiction here? Are only some asked to follow Jesus closely? We know that Martha, Mary, and Lazarus were very close to Jesus, yet they were not numbered among Jesus' constant companions. They lived in Bethany. While it is safe to say that the biblical writers are arguing that commitment to the service of God supersedes all other valid commitments, there are many different ways in which this commitment can unfold.

It is no different today. Not everyone's call to follow Jesus requires leaving one's family. For many people it is precisely within the family that discipleship expresses itself. The point is total commitment. Parents are certainly required to commit themselves wholeheartedly to their children, and adult children often find themselves in similar situations with their aging parents. It may be true that some occupations, by their very nature, demand more of us than do others. Still, regardless of our call in life, discipleship requires unselfish commitment.

We should not overlook the first episode in the gospel passage. There we see James and John, two of Jesus' closest disciples, irate because the people in a Samaritan village did not welcome their ministry. In their anger, they asked that Jesus allow them "to call down fire from heaven to consume them." Jesus said nothing about the Samaritans, but he rebuked his disciples. This shows that full-time ministers are not necessarily more committed than other followers of Jesus. They must always be on their guard against the allure of success and personal aggrandizement.

Paul provides us with some direction for living out our discipleship. He exhorts the early Christians: "Stand firm and do not submit again to the yoke of slavery," and "love your neighbor as yourself." The slavery to which he refers is the erroneous idea that fidelity to the law or to religious practices is what saves, rather than faith in Jesus and a way of life that reflects that faith. Elisha and the individuals in the gospel were directed to put their commitment above even the most cherished values of their cultures; we are directed to do the same. There certainly are values or social customs that tend to yoke us in a kind of slavery. Political and social pressures can result in disdain for those who are different; advertising often perpetuates avaricious consumerism and self-indulgence. And who has not at times felt enslaved by technology? How should a disciple act in such situations?

Paul's second directive needs no interpretation. Love does not mean never having to say you're sorry. It means that we stop "biting and devouring one another." It means that we make peace in our families, at our workplaces, in our country, and in our world. It means that we live lives that "are guided by the Spirit." This is not always easy. The very popular slogan "What would Jesus do?" invites us to look anew at the cost of discipleship in today's world.

Praying with Scripture

- In what ways are you called to be a disciple?

- What has been the cost of this discipleship for you? Are you paying it grudgingly or earnestly?

- Pray that God will give you the willingness and courage to pay the price that discipleship might exact of you.

FOURTEENTH SUNDAY IN ORDINARY TIME
Readings:
Isa 66:10–14c; Ps 66:1–7, 16, 20;
Gal 6:14–18; Luke 10:1–12, 17–20

TWO SIDES OF THE SAME COIN

The readings for today offer us two conflicting images. One is of abundance and rejoicing; the other is of the cross and self-denial. One might think that these two images cannot be harmonized. If we look carefully at their messages, however, we can see how they really do fit together. They are, in fact, two sides of the same coin.

The first reading is from the prophet Isaiah. It is an oracle of salvation, a vision of a joyful future. Through it the prophet announces that the city of Jerusalem, which had been destroyed by the Babylonians and its inhabitants taken into exile or scattered, will be made prosperous again and its people brought back home. The ancient Israelites certainly clung to this promise of future security and happiness. The restoration of the city symbolized the restoration of the entire nation. The scene described in this passage is quite poignant. Jerusalem is depicted as a tender mother, offering her children the comfort and nourishment of her milk. In what some might say is a bold move, the prophet charac-

111

terizes divine comfort as maternal. The language itself invites this particular feminine characterization, for the word for comfort (also translated compassion) comes from the Hebrew for womb. In other words, God shows "womb-love" for the people of Israel.

There are many cities over which we mourn today. Some cities, such as Gaza or Baghdad, have been ravaged by war. Other cities, such as Calcutta and Lagos, are plagued by poverty. We can all name cities in our own country that are riddled with crime. The circumstances of destruction may be different in each case, but many of the inhabitants of these cities can easily identify with the desolate Jerusalem. These ruined cities were their homes, places that they love. The people of today's devastation probably harbor the same hopes and dreams of restoration as did the ancient Israelites. We grieve over such cities, and we pray that, as was the case with the ancient Israelites before them, God will turn their mourning into rejoicing. This is not a vain hope, for as the psalm reminds us, God "changed the sea into dry land; / through the river they passed by foot." God liberated a people before; certainly God can do it again. But how?

The gospel reading provides an answer to this question. The world has an immense need of laborers who will bring the kingdom of God to life. We have read that during Jesus' own lifetime, he sent a group of disciples out into every town and place that he intended to visit. They were to cure the sick and to announce the advent of the reign of God. Like Isaiah before them, their message was one of restoration. The restoration that they announced was more than that of a city or of a single nation, however. The reign of God was for all people, in every time, in every place. An example of the fruitfulness of this mission is Paul. His life exemplifies the description of the apostle found in this reading. He went from city to city announcing the salvific power of the death and resurrection of Jesus. Though he went like a lamb among wolves, he boldly declared: "Let no one make troubles for me; for I bear the marks of Jesus on my body."

Today we are sent to continue this work of announcing the restoration of the people through the gospel of Christ. Today we are the ones with the message: "Peace to this household." "Peace" is a simple greeting to give, but it is a monumental task to accomplish. It involves more than rebuilding cities; it requires rebuilding lives. The first reading suggests that we might accomplish this by taking the broken and desolate people into our arms and our hearts, by comforting them with a compassion like the womb-love of God. We do not have to travel into a foreign country to accomplish this. Genuine world peace really begins in our families and in our neighborhoods. We can, indeed we must, establish it there.

We are the ones who today, through the power of Jesus, can make "even the demons...subject to us." And there are many demons roaming around in our world. There are addictions of every kind, greed under many guises, grudges held for years on end. The transformation of our lives is encompassed in the vision of the rebirth of the city of Jerusalem. We are the new creation of which Paul speaks today. Like Paul, we too must be willing to be crucified to some of the standards of our world, standards that stand in opposition to the reign of God. It is in this way that the cross enters our lives.

Jesus warned us that the message of peace, and the means we employ to establish that peace, might be rejected. Our efforts at change might not always be appreciated. God restored the people in the past, however, and through us, God can continue to restore the people today.

Praying with Scripture

- What concrete actions might you perform for people whose lives have been destroyed?

- Go out of your way this week to show compassion to at least one person.

- Pray that God will make you an instrument of peace in the lives of others.

FIFTEENTH SUNDAY IN ORDINARY TIME

Readings:
Deut 30:10–14; Ps 69:14, 17, 30–31,
33–34, 36–37 (or Ps 19:8–11);
Col 1:15–20; Luke 10:25–37

I Just Love…(Fill in the Blanks)!

Have you ever noticed how often we hear that phrase? I just love to watch the sun set over the lake. I just love the smell of the grease and the hum of the engines. I just love the feeling of being in "the zone." I just love that dress on you. While all of these are genuine and respectable delights, love is much more than any of these pleasures. Genuine love is the most transforming experience we can ever know, and who has ever been transformed by the smell of grease? Or the cut and color of a dress? No, love is much more than any of that!

We often use the word *love* in relation to people and experiences that give us pleasure, but real love usually comes at a great price. The story that Jesus tells in today's gospel points this out to us. The priest and the Levite were on their way to Jerusalem, presumably to fulfill responsibilities in the Temple, privileges that may have been theirs to exercise only a few times a year. They did not know whether the man on the road was dead or alive. If he was dead, they would be responsible for the body, and this would make them ritually unclean and unfit for Temple duty. Concern for another human being meant that they might have to forfeit something that they held dear. It was a risk they did not want to take; it was a price they chose not to pay.

The Samaritan traveler, on the other hand, had no ritual privilege to lose. He was already considered unfit for Temple worship and, therefore, he was despised by those who considered themselves righteous adherents of the Law. But he was filled with concern for another human being, even though under different

114

circumstances that same man might have shunned him. He gave the poor man immediate attention and then paid another person to continue care of him. The Samaritan was willing to pay the price.

In this gospel reading, love of God and love of neighbor seem to be two sides of the same coin. To put it another way, love of God expresses itself in love of others. Why are they so important? Both this gospel and the first reading indicate that love of God and love of others is the law of God. In Hebrew, the word *torah* (law) might be better translated "instruction." We are instructed to love. Moses tells his listeners, however, that such instruction or law is not foreign to us. "It is something very near to you, already in your mouths and in your hearts; you have only to carry it out." Is he suggesting that there is something very human about the law of God? Actually, a careful examination of the content of the Ten Commandments will show that they arise out of human experience. For example, as a community, we should worship together, be truthful, and respect each other's life and property. This in no way minimizes the importance of God's law. Rather, it shows that God's will for us can be found within human experience itself.

Love should be natural to us as well, and in many ways it is. We all seem to have an innate love of the world in which we live with its spectacular sights and scents, its energizing sounds and designs. We also appear to have a natural love for other people. All we have to do is watch how children act toward others—that is, until we teach them otherwise. In many ways we learn what to love and what not to love, which people to love and which ones not to love. The Jewish people learned not to love the Samaritans, and the Samaritans learned to resent the Jews. The priest and the Levite in the gospel story learned to love religious practice more than needy people.

There are various meanings of the word *love*. The love we have for our friends is very different from the love we might have for food, clothing, or the hum of the engine. The Bible too speaks of different kinds of love. The Hebrew word means "commitment" more than it means "emotional attachment." The Greek language has three different words: *'erōs*, which usually refers to passionate love that desires the other for oneself; *philía*, the solicitous love of friends that entails mutual obligations; and *agápē*, which often carries religious meaning and is used in reference to divine love. Because it is not self-seeking, *agápē* is considered love of a higher order. It is said to emphasize neither the passion of *'erōs* nor the warmth of *philía*. This suggests genuine commitment rather than primarily emotional attachment to the other. It should be noted that when Jesus says that we must love, he uses *agápē*. In other words, our love must be based on a desire for the good of the other, not simply passion or affection. This is why Jesus can tell us to "love your enemies" (Luke 6:27, 35).

Praying with Scripture

- In what ways might you be putting service of people above the people themselves?

- Which individuals or groups of people have you excluded from your circle of love? Why? Can you change this?

- Show the people in your life that you love them very much.

SIXTEENTH SUNDAY IN ORDINARY TIME
Readings:
Gen 18:1–10a; Ps 15:2–5;
Col 1:24–28; Luke 10:38–42

MI CASA ES SU CASA

Whenever we travel on vacation, we are dependent on the hospitality of others. We may have to pay for that hospitality, but the quality of their openness to us either enhances or detracts from the enjoyment we experience. Hospitality means that we are made to feel like we are at home. *Mi casa es su casa*; My house is your house! When we feel like we are at home, we want to stay.

In cultures such as the one described in the first reading, hospitality is more than a point of good manners or good business; it is essential for survival. In the ancient world, travelers were vulnerable to the climate and topography of an area not their own, as well as to the inhabitants of the place. Every stranger was a potential enemy. The traveler might be a thief, a murderer, a spy sent ahead to reconnoiter the situation. People had to be on their guard. And travelers never really knew how others would receive them. They could be robbed by their host, captured and enslaved, or put to death. In order to guarantee protection on all sides, a certain protocol of hospitality had to be presumed and observed. The host was expected to treat all travelers as guests, not as potential enemies. Such treatment was thought to neutralize any threat to the household. The traveler was expected to act as a guest rather than a threat, accepting the generosity of the host for necessary food, drink, and shelter. Such hospitality was a temporary arrangement, but it assured everyone of a certain degree of safety.

Today's reading from Genesis illustrates this ancient practice of hospitality. Abraham runs to greet three strangers who have come from the desert, thus initiating the protocol. He attends to their immediate needs, thus demonstrating his openness to them and assuring himself of their kind response. But there is something unique about this story. The men who approach Abraham's tent are not ordinary travelers. This section of the broader biblical story does not inform us who these men are, but it does tell us that one of them foretells the birth of a son to Abraham and Sarah. Who would have such knowledge? Surely someone acting as a messenger of God. The point of the story is captured in a passage from the Letter to the Hebrews: "Do not neglect hospitality, for through it some have unknowingly entertained angels" (Heb 13:2).

We find another example of hospitality in the gospel story. Martha is the one who welcomed Jesus, which means that she was probably the householder, responsible for showing hospitality—which she certainly did. Mary, on the other hand, entertained the guest. Martha is indignant with Mary for not helping her. This should not be seen simply as a sign of peevishness, as so many interpreters suggest. Martha was concerned with service. The word used here is *diakonia*, a word that had ministerial connotations in the early Christian community. In other words, Martha is a faithful disciple. And what is Mary doing? She is seated at Jesus' feet, the customary place of a disciple, and she is listening to his words, a technical phrase that connotes either the fundamental proclamation of the good news or the instruction that flows from it. Mary too is a faithful disciple.

What is going on in this passage? How can both women be considered faithful disciples, yet one of them is said to have chosen "the better part"? As we find so often in the teaching of Jesus, in this story human priorities seem to be turned upside down. Jesus accepts the hospitality of Martha; he never criticizes her for what she is doing in extending it to him. It is only when she seems to be insisting that her sister practice the same kind of discipleship as she has that Jesus says anything to her. It is then that he insists that there is something even more important than hospitality or any other form of service. It is commitment to him. In no way is Jesus implying that *diakonia* is unimportant. It is good, but attending to him is considered "the better part."

What might these readings have to say to us today who are not dependent on hospitality for survival, or who might wonder why Mary's attention to Jesus was chosen over Martha's service? First, we are certainly called to be hospitable or open to others, not only with our homes or goods, but also with our very persons. Attending to the needs of others out of genuine care is certainly at the heart of Christian service. Second, this openness should spring from our commitment to Jesus, not merely from a sense of duty or from any form of self-satisfaction. As we all know, service of others can sometimes flow from selfish motives. When we are truly committed to Jesus, however, it will make little difference whether we serve like Martha did, or sit in rapt attention at the feet of Jesus like Mary. We will be doing God's will for us.

Praying with Scripture

- Think about ways in which you might show hospitality to others.

- Do you see yourself primarily as a "Martha" or as a "Mary"? Does this influence your relationship with others?

- What is your motivation for doing the good that you do?

SEVENTEENTH SUNDAY IN ORDINARY TIME

Readings:
Gen 18:20–32; Ps 138:1–3, 6–8;
Col 2:12–14; Luke 11:1–13

LET US PRAY

I have a distinct memory of my mother teaching me how to pray the rosary. It was a Sunday morning, and I had just stepped out of the house on my way to 9:00 a.m. Mass. I already knew the prayers involved; I just did not know which ones were said on which beads. I also have memories of my father sitting on the edge of our bed with my sister and me at each of his knees saying our nightly prayers. I have no idea why I remember these particular episodes from my childhood. I don't remember my parents teaching me how to eat or how to read, but I do remember them teaching me how to say my prayers.

Just what is prayer? Tomes have been written to answer this question. The *Baltimore Catechism* stated: "Prayer is the lifting of our minds and hearts to God." The catechism further states that petition is not the only kind of prayer. There is also prayer of adoration in which we praise God's glory; prayer of thanksgiving in which we express our gratitude for God's goodness toward us; and prayer of forgiveness for our offenses against that goodness.

Probably the simplest definition for prayer is: "talking with God"—talking *with* God, not merely talking *to* God. Saying prayers is a very good start, but it is only part of the exchange. This definition of prayer says that God speaks to us as well. How can we be sure that what we think is God talking to us is not simply our own imagination working overtime? We probably can't be sure, but that should not deter us from lifting our minds and hearts to God. Still, there are times when we feel that God is not listening, or is not interested, or that God totally rejects what we are saying.

119

The gospel tells us what to do at times when it does not seem that our prayer is being heard. Like the man in the story, we are encouraged to keep knocking on the door. Jesus assures us that our prayers to God will be heard. This assurance is grounded in God's love for us. After all, if loving parents shower their children with everything good, how much more will God give us what is good for us. This raises another issue. We may not always receive that for which we pray; instead, something entirely different may come our way. Some people deal with possible disappointment in this matter by saying: "I asked something of God, and God's answer was no!" Such a statement is not really helpful, for it casts God in a very human and almost unsympathetic light. While prayer of petition is an acknowledgment of our total dependence on God—a religious disposition to be applauded—prayer itself should not be seen as a quid pro quo exchange (I ask; you give).

We must never stop turning to God in our need, but we can only stand patiently and await God's response. Yet, we should remember that petition is only one form of prayer. There is also prayer of praise, thanksgiving, and contrition. These other prayers might be seen as our response to God, who has spoken to us before we even think to pray. God speaks through the marvels of creation, and we burst forth in praise; God speaks through the blessedness of the people and events of our lives, and we express our gratitude; when we have been unfaithful to our covenant commitment, God calls us back, and we repent.

The first reading, a selection from the Book of Genesis, provides us with another picture of prayer. Concerned about the fate of Sodom and Gomorrah, Abraham pleads that those cities be spared for the sake of their innocent inhabitants. Both this story and the gospel account underscore several very important aspects of prayer. First is a deep and abiding trust in God. Abraham would not have pleaded with God nor would the man in the gospel have turned to a friend if they did not think that their petitions would have been granted. Second, both men demonstrate perseverance in prayer even in the face of apparent obstacles. Finally, both stories reveal genuine solicitude for the welfare of others.

Perhaps prayer is a problem for us, not because God does not seem to respond to our petitions, but because we do not respond to God, who is continually speaking to us through the blessings already bestowed on us. In the passage from the Letter to the Colossians, Paul describes the basis and depth of these blessings. He insists that God did not save us in Christ because we deserved it, but because God loves us. In fact, God showered these blessings on us. Even when we were dead because of sin, God brought us to life. Our prayer, whether of praise, gratitude, repentance, or petition, should be our response to this prodigious love.

Praying with Scripture

- Stand in awe of the beauty of the world within which you live and the goodness of the people in your life.

- Spend some time reflecting on the principal blessings that you have already received from God. Allow your heart to be grateful.

- Ask forgiveness for the selfishness in your life.

EIGHTEENTH SUNDAY IN ORDINARY TIME
Readings:
Eccl 1:2; 2:21–23; Ps 90:3–6, 12–14, 17; Col 3:1–5, 9–11; Luke 12:13–21

HERE TODAY AND GONE TOMORROW!

"Vanity of vanities! All things are vanity!" At first glance, this well-known saying from the Book of Ecclesiastes sounds very pessimistic. Some might say that the rest of that biblical book gets even worse, but such an evaluation is a misreading of a very sobering yet genuine perspective on life's pursuits, though not on life itself. This phrase from the ancient sage, the responsorial psalm for today, and the story in the gospel underscore what we all know so well from experience, namely, that everything and everyone is here today and gone tomorrow. Because of this fact, the author of Ecclesiastes insists that the meaning of life cannot be found in possessions that do not last.

This is a hard saying in a world such as ours where our personal value is often measured by the extent and quality of our possessions. Those who are admired are the people who have money; those who have power are the people who have money; those who set so many of the standards of society are the people who have money. Qoheleth, the teacher in the Book of Ecclesiastes, says that this is all vanity, emptiness, futility. The Hebrew word for vanity might be better translated "lacking in substance." According to Qoheleth, the admiration of others, the power, and the influence all lack substance; they are here today and gone tomorrow.

Today's gospel reading contains a similar message. In it, Jesus tells a parable of a rich man who thought about nothing but enlarging his barns for the overflowing harvests he was expecting. There is no indication that this man gained his wealth dishonestly; nor does the parable say that he manipulated or oppressed his workers. The point being made addresses the question of values. According to Jesus, this man was a fool because he invested all of himself in a treasure that would be of little use to him when he died. There is an implication here that he was "not rich in what matters to God." Jesus used the parable to underscore the vanity or folly of greed.

Paul directs our attention to the treasures that really endure. In the passage from the Letter to the Colossians, he admonishes us to seek what is above, not what is of the earth and will not endure. What does this really mean to us in the everyday events of life? Actually, Paul's exhortation to put to death "immorality, impurity, passion, evil desire, and the greed that is idolatry" and to "stop lying to one another" hits home as if he had our world in mind when he first spoke these words. Our world caters to our desire for immediate gratification of every kind. It encourages us to amass as many possessions as possible. In so many ways this point of view thrives on deceit. Neither Qoheleth nor Jesus nor Paul would say that life on earth is meaningless. Rather, they all insist that one cannot find life's real meaning in possessions. To think that way is foolish.

Paul reminds us that, through our baptism, we have been brought into the power of Jesus' death and resurrection. In this way we died to a life lacking in substance, and we were raised with him to a new life, a life with substance. We "have put on the new self, which is being renewed...in the image of its creator." Power and influence and possessions come and go, but this new self will endure because it is grounded in the power of the Risen Lord. We are now expected to live moral and upright lives in a world that fosters immorality of every kind; we are now called to be generous with our possessions, our time, and ourselves in a world that applauds greed and selfishness; we are now required to be honest in our dealings with one another in a world devoured by every form of deceit.

So many of the pursuits of life today are vain, empty, lacking in substance. Our culture idolizes youth, money, pleasure, and a carefree style of living. Yet we all know that such pursuits are very tenuous. Youth certainly does not last long for anyone. Financial stability is out of the reach of many, and those who are able to enjoy it know that it does not take much for such stability to be threatened, even turned upside down. Pleasure itself is like a ravenous beast that is seldom satisfied, and people who can afford to enjoy a carefree style of living tell us that they often tire of it or grow out of it. If we look deep into ourselves, we will have to admit that the human heart longs for something more permanent, more lasting. We will soon come to see that we have been made for "what is above" and that the desires of the human heart cannot be satisfied by what is here today and gone tomorrow.

Praying with Scripture

- To what extent do you think that you have conformed to the fleeting standards of this culture?

- Which of your possessions would you find most difficult to relinquish? What might this say about you?

- Pray for the wisdom to cherish what is meaningful in life.

NINETEENTH SUNDAY IN ORDINARY TIME
Readings:
Wis 18:6–9; Ps 33:1, 12, 18–22;
Heb 11:1–2, 8–19; Luke 12:32–48

SEEING IS BELIEVING! REALLY?

The phrase "seeing is believing" is well known to us all. It suggests skepticism; it implies that we will not accept the truth of something unless we can somehow see it ourselves. While the phrase may validly express a concern for verification, it contradicts basic religious faith. To paraphrase the writer of the Letter to the Hebrews: Not seeing is believing. This phrase may, at first, be difficult to grasp? But then, so is real faith.

The author of the Letter to the Hebrews turns to Abraham as a perfect example of such faith. Without knowing exactly what he would find as he followed the inspiration of God, Abraham left his home of origin and journeyed to a foreign land. Abraham did not see what was ahead of him, yet he believed. Down through the centuries, migrants of every nation have known the uncertainty and fear that accompanies such a step. In their case, faith alone spurred them on. Abraham clung tenaciously to God's promise of descendants, though to him such a promise seemed to be an impossibility. He did not see how the promise could be fulfilled, yet he believed. Childless couples cling to a similar hope, despite the fact that no promise has been made to them. The greatest test of his faith came to Abraham when he was asked by God to sacrifice the very child who was to fulfill that promise of descendants. In being willing to sacrifice this child, Abraham showed that he was willing to relinquish not only his son, but also the future of his entire household. He perfectly exemplifies the adage: "Faith is the realization of what is hoped for and evidence of things not seen."

The instructions given by Jesus in the gospel require the same kind of faith. The focus there is not the seeming incredibility of the object of faith, however, but the need to cling to that faith even when its fulfillment is long in coming. The followers of Jesus are told not to seek security in the realities of this world, but to look for it in the treasures that belong to the reign of God. Jesus then exhorts them to be steadfast in their faith, and he provides a story to explain what he means. Servants were entrusted with the management of a household. No one knew just when the house-holder would return. Therefore, a wise servant would be ever vigilant, since the householder could return at any moment and would expect to find everything in order and all awaiting his reappearance. "Faith is the realization of what is hoped for and evidence of things not seen."

If faith is not based on what is seen, then on what is it based? Each of today's readings suggests that the foundation of such faith is the trustworthiness of God, who has generously blessed these same people in the past. The author of the Book of Wisdom encouraged the people of his time by reminding them of how God had protected their ancestors as they escaped from Egyptian bondage. They took courage in the "sure knowledge of the oaths [of God] in which they put their faith." God's faithfulness to Abraham is invoked to strengthen the faith of the Christians to whom the Letter to the Hebrews was sent. It was because of this faith that "the ancients were well attested." Writing to his community of Christians, Luke recounts how Jesus instructed his followers to be steadfast: "Do not be afraid any longer, little flock, for your Father is pleased to give you the kingdom." In many ways, the faith that is handed down from the past is grounded in the goodness of God shown in that same past.

Like believers of long ago, we too have been called to cling to the hope of a future that may seem too good to be true. We live in a world of unimaginable insecurity. Millions of people have been torn from their homes, driven out into the world with nowhere to go. Unlike Abraham, they were not promised a new home. In what or in whom can their faith be based? Vast populations have been stamped out as a result of genocide or pandemics like AIDS. For these people, there is no promise of descendants. How will these households be rebuilt? And what can be said about the countless people who languish under the thumbs of oppressive governments? How will they be led to freedom?

The gospel provides answers to these questions. The reign of God has been entrusted to us. Today we are the stewards in charge of the household, who "distribute the food allowance at the proper time." We are the ones called to provide shelter for the homeless, new life for the desperate, freedom for the oppressed. We must be the sign of faith in today's world. Can we believe this? Will we pass the test of faith?

Praying with Scripture

- On which past blessings does your faith in God rest?
- How might you be a better steward of the treasures of the household of God?
- Pray for the strength to be steadfast in holding to your faith, particularly in times of great challenge.

TWENTIETH SUNDAY IN ORDINARY TIME
Readings:
Jer 38:4–6, 8–10; Ps 40:2–4, 18;
Heb 12:1–4; Luke 12:49–53

THE TRUTH MAY SET YOU FREE, BUT AT WHAT COST?

As we were growing up, we were all taught to tell the truth. But we soon learned that, just as there were consequences for telling a lie, telling the truth sometimes produced unpleasant results. Not only might we have been made to face the music ourselves, but in being honest we might have implicated others as well, and no one likes a tattletale. Still, no society can survive without the truth, regardless of what it might cost. We have to be able to trust one another, and we have to be strong enough to accept the truth about ourselves and our society. Otherwise, we will not be able to remedy what could prevent growth and improvement. Several weeks ago (Sixteenth Sunday of Ordinary Time) we reflected on the cost of discipleship. The readings for this Sunday invite us to look at that theme again, but this time from a slightly different perspective. In both the passage from the prophet Jeremiah and the gospel reading, we find examples of the cost of telling the truth. In both instances, this cost is quite high.

In the first reading, we find Jeremiah imprisoned. What was his crime? He was advising the soldiers, in whose custody he had been placed, that the city of Jerusalem was doomed and that any protection they might offer it would be pointless. Better simply to surrender. Besides, the defeat of the city would be God's way of punishing the people for their infidelity. The officials of the court told the king that "he is demoralizing the soldiers who are left in this city." As a result, Jeremiah was thrown into a cistern, an ancient form of solitary confinement. Was Jeremiah honestly announcing the truth of God's word? Or was he guilty of treason? At times of political unrest, such a question is difficult to answer. Regardless of how one interprets Jeremiah's situation, for telling the truth as he understood it the prophet was made to pay the price exacted of an act of treason.

This is a tragic picture, not only because of the consequences Jeremiah was forced to endure, but also because of the personality of the man himself. He did not consider himself a fit subject for the office of prophet. In fact, he tried to evade his call, giving excuses for why he would not be able to meet its demands (Jer 1:6). Many commentators refer to Jeremiah as "the reluctant prophet," the one whose disposition was too tender for the misery that he would have to face. He had to warn his own people that they were going to be defeated by their mortal enemies the Babylonians, and it fell to him to proclaim the destruction of the city that he loved and the Temple that he cherished. Telling the truth must have broken his heart.

In the gospel account, Jesus describes his own role as that of setting "the earth on fire." While on the one hand this expression could suggest that Jesus is aflame with zeal for establishing the reign of God, on the other hand, the tone of the rest of the passage implies that it points to great suffering. We often think of Jesus as a man of peace, and rightly so. He did go around the countryside to the villages of the land, announcing comfort and relief to those in need, but he realized that his message of reform and rebirth would not be accepted by all. It could mean division. Today's gospel reading tells us that such division would be felt at the very core of society, in the family unit.

In order to realize the depth and severity of such a rupture, we must remember how essential kinship loyalty was in the ancient world. In that world societies were community-oriented, unlike the individual-oriented perspective most of us cherish today. Individuals could not survive alone, and what linked them to the broader community was the kinship structure. In today's reading, Jesus acknowledges that the truth of his teaching would cause some within the family to accept him, while others would not. This resulted in actual alienation of family members and the possibility of their being ostracized from their community of origin.

Standing for the truth is no easier today than it was for Jeremiah or for the early followers of Jesus. In many parts of the world, it may still place people in jeopardy for their lives. Nor is it uncommon that individuals must sometimes choose between the truth as they see it and family solidarity. Most of us do not face such drastic circumstances, however. Still, we may have to pay a price for standing for the truth. We might be opposed to a political policy and, as a result, be accused of being unpatriotic. It could be that something at our workplace should be challenged, and we might have to risk being labeled uncooperative. Or, following our conscience could put us at odds with friends or family. The truth may set us free, but at what cost?

Praying with Scripture

- Who are the people you know who stand up for the truth regardless of the price they may have to pay? Tell them how much you appreciate their honesty and courage.

- For which truths are you willing to stand up? Why are these truths so important to you?

- Pray for the grace to be a person of conviction.

TWENTY-FIRST SUNDAY IN ORDINARY TIME
Readings:
Isa 66:18–21; Ps 117:1–2;
Heb 12:5–7, 11–13; Luke 13:22–30

ALL ARE GOD'S PEOPLE

As surprising as it may seem, there is a divine characteristic that many religious people find very troublesome. It is God's universal concern for all the people of the world. It seems that some people resent the thought that God would be gracious toward people who hold different religious and political views. They prefer to see such people punished for their errors rather than accepted by God and even saved.

This exclusionary point of view can be found in some of the earliest traditions of Israel. There we find the notion of a patron God who chose one people from among many, protected them from threats posed by other nations, and blessed them with peace and prosperity. Such a God was considered the special patron of Israel, but not the patron of the entire world. The other nations had their own gods to care for them. It was only gradually that the perception of God developed and expanded so that the universal scope of God's love and care became clear. The Israelites soon came to see that God is concerned with the happiness and salvation of all. Today's readings underscore this universal divine concern.

The passage from the Book of Isaiah contains an announcement that in the near future people from several foreign lands will be called together by God. These gathered people will become a sign of the glory of God for still other foreigners. This is a very curious prediction. It is one thing to bring the captive and scattered Israelites back to their land, but those referred to here are not Israelites. These people come from the "nations of every language." In other words, those who are outsiders will become insiders. To this remarkable example of divine universalism is added the shocking declaration that these foreigners will even be numbered among the priests and Levites. Has ancient Israel's strict code of purity, particularly ritual purity, been overturned? Will the unclean foreigners gain access even to Israel's most sacred precincts? Has the exclusive circle known as the people of God been expanded to include anyone who wishes to join? And if this is the case, who now does not belong to the people of God?

The gospel reveals a slightly different perspective of the notion of being chosen. Its focus is on entrance into the reign of God. Some of the people at the time of Jesus seemed to have presumed that since as Jews they belonged to the chosen people, they would automatically have easy access to the long-awaited reign of God. This reign was understood as a promised state of being that would bring to fulfillment all of Israel's religious hopes and dreams. Jesus quickly disabused the people of their erroneous presumption. He insisted that those who would not make the necessary effort would be denied entrance into the reign of God. And who would occupy the places they thought would be theirs? As was seen in the passage from Isaiah, it will be foreigners "from the east and the west and from the north and the south." Once again we see that outsiders will become insiders. But there is an added reversal in the gospel reading: Jesus warns that those who had been considered insiders might find themselves outside the banquet.

Though it consists of only two short verses, the responsorial psalm picks up this same theme of universal inclusion. In it, all nations, all peoples are invited to praise God. The reason given for this praise is the divine kindness and fidelity (two technical covenant words) shown to Israel. This call to foreigners to praise a God not their own may seem strange. We must remember, however, that Israel was a rather insignificant nation in the ancient world. If other nations realized that despite this lowly status Israel's God was able to protect and care for the people, these other nations would recognize the power and goodness of that God. Thus, through the witness of Israel, other nations would be drawn to God and would join Israel in praising God.

One aspect of being an insider is not always appreciated, and that is the need to be disciplined. If we truly want to belong to the reign of God, we must act accordingly. The author of the Letter to the Hebrews calls our attention to this. We must be trained in righteousness, and this is not always pleasant. Many of us need to rid ourselves of selfishness and arrogance. Others of us need to cleanse our hearts of bias and discrimination. The other readings and the psalm response provide challenges for us as well. Our baptism conferred on us the responsibility of witnessing to the entire world the glory of God. People of every religious faith should be able to recognize God's goodness in the way we live our lives and the manner in which we interact with them. This is particularly important today, when there is such animosity among people of differing faiths. This interfaith challenge may well be the narrow gate through which we must pass if we hope to sit at the table in God's kingdom.

Praying with Scripture

- How do you witness the universal love of God to those who embrace a different faith?

- How open are you to accepting others on their own terms?

- What challenge or "discipline" may you be facing in this regard?

TWENTY-SECOND SUNDAY IN ORDINARY TIME
Readings:
Sir 3:17–18, 20, 28–29; Ps 68:4–8, 10–11;
Heb 12:18–19, 22–24a; Luke 14:1, 7–14

"ANYTHING YOU CAN DO, I CAN DO BETTER!"

These are the first words of a clever lyric from the Broadway musical *Annie Get Your Gun*. While the "battle of the sexes" is the original setting for the song, the sentiments expressed fit many more situations. They are explicitly promoted in the arena of competitive sports; they are often the motivation that drives the fashion industry; and they are probably most obvious in the field of advertising. In venues such as these, it is apparently not enough to be good; one has to be better or, ideally, one should be the best.

If you want to make it in the world today, you have to advertise. If you have a product to sell or a service to offer, you must make it known, and you must brag about it. In order to showcase their product, many advertisers claim: "We have what no one else has!" "Our product is bigger and better and lasts longer!" "We can do what no one else can do!" "We are more reliable than the rest!" Face it—a humble attitude will probably not make you Number One in any field. Does this mean that we believers should not strive to be better, to produce better products, or advertise? Must we refrain from extolling the benefits of what we might have to offer? Not at all. It simply suggests that it is very difficult to be humble in such circumstances.

The reading from Sirach is a short discourse on humility. In it, the author admonishes the student ("my child") to learn to live within the realm of possibility. In other words, accept yourself as you are; don't seek what is too sublime for you or search for things beyond your strength. There is a very thin line here between being content with the abilities that we have and simply sliding through life with as little effort as possible. This advice is certainly not suggesting that we should not try to excel—but there is a difference between working as hard as we can in order to be the best that we can be and presuming that we are more than we really are. Nor do we always discover that thin line or recognize that difference. Actually, humility is more a disposition of the soul than it is a course of action.

The parable that Jesus tells does not condemn excellence but arrogance. It demonstrates how people with inflated egos often assume places of honor. In doing so, they risk having to relinquish those places in favor of someone who is more distinguished than they are. Instead of proudly glorying in their own importance, they are then made to feel ashamed. There is no place for an "I am better than you" attitude among the followers of the one who in his humanity emptied himself of the privileges of divinity. We may indeed have an abundance of material possessions or a fine education or exceptional talent. Still, these do not mean that we are superior to others. Those who are so fortunate would do well to heed the admonition of Sirach: "Humble yourself the more, the greater you are." Such humility is really honesty, for everything we have is a gift from God. No one did anything to earn special blessings.

In many other ways we try to impress others with our importance. We might act in a way that generates praise and acceptance, or we might choose to associate only with important people. We want to be known as having read the key books, as frequenting the popular places, as being invited to the important parties. And equally significant is the fact that influential people come to our parties, or at least recognize us. We deceive ourselves when we think that any of this makes us important. Though Jesus does not say anything about reading books or visiting places, what he says about parties clearly addresses this matter: "When you hold a banquet, invite the poor, the crippled, the lame, the blind." Invite those whose presence cannot enhance your own prestige; invite those who cannot repay you in kind.

So much of our time and energy is wasted in trying to convince others of our importance. Besides, most of us will not be featured in the society pages regardless of what we do. Jesus points to what is really of value, and that is caring for those in need of our help. Is not this what so many of us do anyway? We care for family members and friends and neighbors; we offer our time and whatever resources we can to soup kitchens and clothing drives; we join walks and runs in support of worthy causes. We are just ordinary people attentive to others in ordinary ways that are really extraordinary. In such situations, we do not claim places of honor; we do not insist on special recognition. Though we may not be conscious of it, in such situations we really conduct our affairs in genuine humility and not so that we are seen to be doing the right things.

Praying with Scripture

- On occasion we all perform for the approval of others. Pray for the grace to recognize this in yourself and to change.

- How might you be more attentive to those who are genuinely needy?

- Perform at least one act of kindness that will be unobserved by others.

TWENTY-THIRD SUNDAY IN ORDINARY TIME
Readings:
Wis 9:13–18b; Ps 90:3–6, 12–17;
Phlm 9–10, 12–17; Luke 14:25–33

DECISIONS, DECISIONS, DECISIONS!

When I was much younger, I used to think that being obedient was hard. As I got older I came to realize that obeying others may be unpleasant, but I don't think it is really difficult. At least in such situations I know what is expected of me. Becoming an adult means that you have to make decisions for yourself. Now *that* is hard! This is particularly true in situations in which there are so many options from which one might choose. Ours is a world characterized by multiple choices. Many young people enroll in college without having decided upon a major, and it may be several semesters before they do choose one. The shelves of our markets are filled with many brands of the same product, all of which claim to be the best of its kind. And who can fathom the countless cable stations that are available to us at the flick of the remote? Decisions, decisions, decisions! If only someone would just tell us which to choose!

Every society has a wisdom tradition, a treasury of insights gleaned from experience that sets a direction for living in such a way as to ensure success and well-being. Those who are wise have learned from this tradition, and they also contribute to it from their own reflection on the experience of life. All of the readings for this Sunday focus on some aspect of the wisdom of our religious ancestors, a wisdom that has been handed down to us through the teachings of our faith.

The reading from the Book of Wisdom clearly states the ambiguity that human beings face. Our deliberations are timid; our plans are unsure. This is because we often make choices that do not flow from noble aspirations. We are selfish or cruel; we are arrogant or dishonest; we are ignorant and inexperienced. Our human limitations can be a burden, and we need divine guidance. But even in seeking this guidance, we can so easily be deceived by our own ego. If "scarce do we guess the things on earth," how can we hope to grasp the ways of God? "Who can conceive what the Lord intends?" Our desire to comprehend urges us on in the search for wisdom, even though we know we will probably never fully grasp what we seek. Acknowledging this we search nonetheless, and we pray that God will bestow the necessary wisdom upon us.

The second reading sketches a situation in which Philemon is invited to make a serious decision. A slave by the name of Onesimus has run away from his master and has found an advocate in Paul. Having established a relationship with this slave, Paul asks Philemon to set aside his rights and position as a slaveholder and to act in accord with the true equality established among believers through baptism. Paul's arguments are quite forceful. Still, the decision is Philemon's. Though he has a right to decide either way, Paul urges him to be influenced more by his religious tradition than by the societal norms.

In the gospel account Jesus calls for a most radical decision. He offers his followers options: membership in society based on family ties or membership in a community of faith based on commitment to him. Jesus realizes that this is asking much of one for whom kinship ties are the basis of both personal and societal identity. Severing these ties must have felt like disowning one's family and history. Realizing the pain involved in this decision, Jesus states: "Whoever does not carry [one's] own cross and come after me cannot be my disciple." The seriousness of this decision prompts us to consider whether or not we have what it takes to make it. In this regard, Jesus offers two examples of assessing the necessary provisions. One does not embark on building projects without first taking stock of the available materials. Otherwise, one risks having to halt construction before it has been completed. In like manner, one must be prepared to follow Jesus lest the requirements of this decision become more than one can meet.

The way of life to which believers have been called may appear to be foolishness if judged by the standards of the world, but it really embodies wisdom and insight. From among all the opportunities placed before us, we must decide which will make us better people, which will enhance the lives of others, and which will improve the world in which we live. Jesus directs us to think things through before we make our decisions. The author of Wisdom tells us to ask for enlightenment from God. Whichever the decision we do make, it should flow from our religious values, what the author of Wisdom calls "things [that] are in heaven." We are called to make decisions as disciples of Jesus, not as foolish people caught up in the many shallow values of our time.

Praying with Scripture

- How often do you pause in prayerful reflection before making an important decision?

- By which standards and values do you usually determine your course of action—those of contemporary society or those of our religious tradition?

- Are your ties to the people of God as strong as the ties that bind you to your family?

TWENTY-FOURTH SUNDAY IN ORDINARY TIME
Readings:
Exod 32:7-11, 13-14; Ps 51:3-4, 12-13, 17, 19;
1 Tim 1:12-17; Luke 15:1-32

WE DON'T ALWAYS GET WHAT WE DESERVE!

At first glance, ancient Israel's insistence on being the chosen people of God may appear to be somewhat arrogant. A closer look reveals, however, that again and again the people admitted that though they firmly believed that they had indeed been specially chosen by God, they did not merit this distinction. Far from it! In fact, they were quick to own up to their own limitations and inconstancy. They admitted that they were a fickle, sinful people, undeserving of God's love and care. And yet, out of pure graciousness on God's part, the blessings of this distinction accompanied them every step of their way. They may not have been a loyal people, but God had always been a merciful God. Divine mercy was particularly evident when the people were most unfaithful. God always gave them another chance.

Today's reading from Exodus illustrates this. While Moses was on the mountain communing with God, the people were in the camp below. They became impatient with Moses' delay and prevailed upon Aaron to construct some kind of religious icon for them to worship. They had only recently been delivered by God from the hand of the Egyptians, and here they are, not only irritated but itching for some religious symbol, any religious symbol, to worship. The wrath of God's fury blazed against them. And who would blame God for destroying them? But Moses interceded for them, and God relented. In fact, rather than punish them, God promised them numerous descendants and a rich land on which to live. They certainly did not get what they deserved.

In so many ways, we are not very different from them. We have been called into a loving relationship with a God who has given us everything we need to live meaningful and productive lives. And yet we too "have turned aside from the way [God] pointed out to [us]"; we too are a "stiff-necked" people. And how does God treat us in our sinfulness? As with the people of ancient Israel, God is merciful toward us. Rather than destroy us, God relents of punishing us. Like those who went before us, we are given chance after chance to return to the embrace of a loving God. In other words, we do not always get what we deserve.

Paul certainly knew the mercy of God. He himself tells us that before his conversion he had persecuted those who believed in Jesus. Once he had met the Risen Lord he became one of his most devoted followers. And like his Israelite ancestors, Paul was not afraid to boast. He did not boast of his own strengths and accomplishments, however; he insisted that he had been strengthened by Christ Jesus and had been found to be trustworthy. Again, Paul was quick to insist that it was the mercy of God that made him trustworthy. Paul would be the first to admit that he didn't get what he deserved.

Jesus speaks emphatically about divine mercy, about God, who not only forgives sinners but also actually goes out and looks for them. He then tells three stories that illustrate the extent of divine mercy. In the first story, God is depicted as a shepherd who will leave an entire flock in order to search for the one sheep that may have wandered off. In the second, God is characterized as a woman who lost a single coin and sweeps the entire house until she finds it. The third story is probably the best known. It may well be the most shocking parable of the entire gospel tradition. Known as the story of the prodigal son, it might better be titled "the prodigal father," because its underlying theme is the mercy and love of the father.

In each of these parables there is rejoicing when what was lost is finally found. This rejoicing is an indication of the value the shepherd, the woman, and the father placed on what had been lost. It should be noted that this was not a private rejoicing. Friends and neighbors were invited to join the celebrations. This aspect of the story of the prodigal is very important, for the obedient son refused to participate. In fact, he was resentful that there was a celebration at all. It is clear that the father [God] appears to be more concerned with the fate of the sinner than with the reward for those who have been faithful. This is often troubling for people who have lived righteous lives, for it points to the resentment that they sometimes feel when people who have not been faithful are granted the same blessings as those, like themselves, who have been.

The mercy of God is a difficult teaching to accept if we judge ourselves, over against others, to be righteous and deserving of reward. Actually, we should find the message for today very comforting. God is eager to be merciful toward us, not vengeful and punishing. This is definitely good news, reason to celebrate and rejoice. Indeed, we don't always get what we deserve.

Praying with Scripture

- Are you resentful when others seem to avoid just punishment? Does this flow from a sense of justice or from envy?

- Pray for the grace to forgive those who in some way may have offended or harmed you.

- Pray for the strength to admit your own mistakes.

TWENTY-FIFTH SUNDAY IN ORDINARY TIME
Readings:
Amos 8:4–7; Ps 113:1–2, 4–8; 1 Tim 2:1–8; Luke 16:1–13

$$$$$

It is very difficult to talk about financial equity in a market-driven economy. Some entertainers and sports figures earn extravagant salaries, while people in essential service professions such as teaching often find it difficult to make ends meet. So many people struggle with some form of money problem. In the broader scope of world economy, however, citizens of this country are considered some of the most privileged in the world. If we were to follow the gospel injunction to sell what we have and give to the poor, we would all have to go on welfare and would become someone else's financial burden. So what are we supposed to do?

The Bible never really tells us *what* to do. Instead, it provides standards that suggest *how* we are to do what we decide. We see this in today's reading from Amos. The prophet is speaking to the wealthy who live in the prosperous northern kingdom. He does not condemn prosperity itself, but the way they use the power that comes from wealth. Rather than take care of the less fortunate in their midst, they take advantage of them for their own benefit. We must remember that the people of ancient Israel were bound together by covenant. This arrangement implies that the wealthy had covenant responsibilities to the needy. Caring for the poor of the land was not a question of charity; it was a matter of covenant justice.

The gospel reading is rather difficult to understand. A man who first squandered the property of his employer and then hoodwinked him out of goods that were due him is actually praised by the very employer he outmaneuvered. A closer look will reveal that the steward was praised for his prudence (the Greek word means practical wisdom), not for his dishonesty.

The ancients had developed an economic system very different from what we have today, and so we cannot judge the steward by contemporary standards. The story does not tell us what debts were forgiven. They might have been the overcharge that enhanced the employer's holdings at the expense of the debtors, or they could have been the commission that the steward would have taken off the top. Whatever the case, the steward did not manage his employer's property well, but he certainly knew how to endear himself to the debtors, thus taking care of himself. In this he showed self-interested practical wisdom. It is precisely this practical wisdom that Jesus holds up to the children of light. Like the steward, they are expected to exercise this kind of wisdom. But while the steward was devious, they are to be trustworthy, even in matters that pertain to this world, for

"The person who is trustworthy in very small matters is also trustworthy in great ones."

We might better understand this passage if we look at the meaning of some of the Greek words. Two important words in today's gospel are derived from *oíkos*, the Greek word for household: steward or household manager (*oikonómos*); and household servant (*oikétes*). Neither the steward nor the household servant can claim ownership of the goods of the household. Jesus' last words state: "You cannot serve both God and mammon." "Serve" means be to be a slave to something. In this passage "dishonest wealth" and "mammon" are translations of the same Greek word. Jesus is saying that we have to choose between God and riches dishonestly acquired.

Another word derived from *oíkos* (household), though not found in the story but important for our consideration, is *oikonomía* (economy or household management). The word has broadened to include even the largest human communities. Our contemporary economy is not only market driven, but it is also based on principles of private property. As valuable as these principles may be, they often blur some of the values raised in today's readings. Besides, though we have a right to private property, we know that we really only use, rather than own, the goods of the earth. They are not our exclusive property. Pope John Paul II speaks of the "social mortgage" on all our possessions.

Using the language of the gospel, we might say that the earth with all its riches is the household; God is the householder; and we are the stewards or household servants. The question is: Just how do we manage the goods that are in our trust? Are we devious? Or are we trustworthy? Do we manage these goods in ways that enhance the entire household and benefit all who belong? Or do we squander them, thinking only of ourselves? And when we are called to accountability, do we change our course of action? Or do we finagle ways that will guarantee our own comfort, even at the expense of others? Do we cling to the rights of private property? Or do we recognize our covenant responsibility in seeing to the just needs of others?

Jesus' last words are very demanding: "You cannot be a [slave] to both God and [dishonest wealth]." The decision is left to us.

Praying with Scripture

- How possessive are you of the goods that are yours?

- In what ways might you be more openhanded toward others?

- In what ways do you benefit from our economic system, while others suffer from it? What responsibility might this place on you?

TWENTY-SIXTH SUNDAY IN ORDINARY TIME
Readings:
Amos 6:1a, 4–7; Ps 146:7–10;
1 Tim 6:11–16; Luke 16:19–31

IT'S NONE OF MY BUSINESS!

The phrase *it's none of my business* can mean more than one thing. It can be an acknowledgment that we must respect the right of others to self-determination and personal privacy. Or it can be used as an excuse for not stepping in to help when it is clear that another needs our help. The phrase has almost become a motto for a society in which individuals are so totally absorbed in their own life projects that they fail to consider the common good.

The theme of last Sunday, namely, covenant responsibility of the rich for the poor, is the main focus of this Sunday's reflection as well. Once again the oracle proclaimed by Amos is scathing: "Woe to the complacent in Zion!" The prophet does not condemn the people for their wealth, but for their complacency in the face of the hardships that others are forced to endure. The description of the style of living of the wealthy rivals an episode of *Lifestyles of the Rich and Famous*. They are so busy luxuriating in their opulence that "they are not made ill by the collapse of Joseph," a reference to the fall of the entire northern kingdom of Israel. They are completely unaware of or unconcerned about the plight of other Israelites, compatriots of theirs who are partners in the covenant they made with God.

The gospel reading paints a picture that illustrates the same theme. At first, the rich man enjoys an exceptionally indulgent style of life, while poor Lazarus, covered with sores, lies at the rich man's door, hoping for a few scraps from his table (a scene that is replayed far too frequently in our own cities). This is a graphic example of the rich man's utter disregard for someone in desperate need. As is so often the case in the parables of Jesus, a dramatic reversal of fortune takes place. The one who once was privileged now finds himself in torment, while Lazarus, who previously had been destitute, is now safe in the embrace of Abraham. If the prosperous man is not condemned because of his wealth, why does he suffer such a horrendous fate?

The man's own dialogue with Abraham answers that question. First, since both he and Lazarus have a connection with Abraham, they must be partners in the same covenant. The rich man is told that his brothers should not need an extraordinary revelation from heaven to remind them of their covenant responsibilities. They have Moses and the prophets, a reference to their religious tradition, and this tradition is very clear about the social dimension of the covenant. In order to escape his fate, his brothers have only to follow the dictates of that covenant, one of which is care for those who are in need. As for the rich man, the die is cast. He did not assuage the agony of Lazarus; now it is impossible for Lazarus to provide him the comfort he seeks, for "a great chasm is established to prevent anyone from crossing" from one side to the other.

This is one of the few places in the gospels where divine judgment is described. And the judgment here is quite harsh. In fact, it seems inappropriately harsh. After all, the rich man did not do anything wrong. He did not steal from Lazarus, nor physically assault him; but he had a weighty responsibility toward Lazarus and he failed to fulfill it, and this was a serious sin of omission. The severity of his punishment throws light on the gravity of this responsibility.

It is always difficult to strike the right balance between respecting the space of another and stepping in to help. When should we make someone else's life our business? The complexity of our society makes this balance even more difficult to achieve. This difficulty can be clearly seen within the family. Partners try to negotiate this balance with each other, as do parents with children and children with parents. In the family, this negotiation is not attempted in a vacuum, however; it is done within the embrace of mutual love and concern.

It is a comparable love and concern that bind covenant partners together. The absence of such dispositions explains precisely why Amos castigated the wealthy Israelites, and why the rich man in the gospel ended up in torment in the netherworld. It is the same love and concern that bind us to each other and prompt us to step into another's life in order to offer help. Our own covenant responsibilities extend far beyond the confines of our families or our parish communities. We cannot be deaf to the cries of the needy in far-flung corners of the world. We cannot close our eyes to the plight of the victims of oppression and war. We cannot be complacent while others are collapsing as their lives are being destroyed. The die has not yet been cast for us. We still have time to be faithful to what our religious tradition teaches: The well-being of others is indeed our business.

Praying with Scripture

- What practical steps might you take to secure "justice for the oppressed" (Ps 146:7)?

- Have you ever worked at a food pantry or volunteered at a soup kitchen?

- Pray that you will learn to balance personal financial security with direct assistance to poor persons or funding for social programs for them.

TWENTY-SEVENTH SUNDAY IN ORDINARY TIME
Readings:
Hab 1:2–3; 2:2–4; Ps 95:1–2, 6–9; 2 Tim 1:6–8,13–14; Luke 17:5–10

IS IT FAITH? OR IS IT HOPE? AND DOES IT MATTER?

We don't hear much about faith nowadays, except faith in ourselves. Ours is a culture of self-reliance and self-determination. If we are honest with ourselves, however, we will have to admit that we are all burdened with a measure of self-doubt. Not necessarily the unhealthy kind of self-doubt, but an acknowledgment that we cannot always do whatever we set out to accomplish.

A New Testament writer tells us that "Faith is the realization of what is hoped for" (Heb 11:1). Just what does this mean? The catechism makes clear distinctions between faith and hope. It tells us that faith is belief in divine truths, and hope is trust in God. The Bible does not seem to understand these religious sentiments in quite the same way. In fact, if we look carefully at passages that speak of faith or hope, we will find that faith is actually reliance on or confidence in God, and hope is expectation of a better future.

The readings for today offer us three glimpses into what the Bible means by faith. When the apostles ask Jesus, "Increase our faith," he gives them an example of the power of faith. He claims that even a little bit of it can work marvels. But what it is we are not told. The story that follows is meant to encourage faithfulness, not faith itself. There is a connection between being faithful to one's responsibilities and living by faith, however. If "Faith is the realization of what is hoped for," then perhaps faithfulness means that we continue to live this assurance even in difficult circumstances. Faith, then, is the foundation of faithfulness; and faithfulness strengthens faith.

145

In the second reading, Paul admonishes Timothy to remain steadfast in his testimony to the Lord. The faith of which he speaks is acceptance of Jesus as fulfillment of the promises of God. While there is definitely assurance in this kind of faith, it is more than assurance of things hoped for; it is assurance in what has already taken place, namely, the resurrection of Jesus. This assurance is the basis of Christian commitment. It is because of such assurance that Paul can say: "God did not give us a spirit of cowardice." In other words, faith not only enables us to be faithful, but it strengthens us to be courageous.

The vision of the prophet Habakkuk is one of terror and destruction. The people are already close to despair. The prophet exclaims in agony: "How long, O LORD? I cry for help / but you do not listen!" There are no words of comfort in this passage. Instead, the prophet is told to write down the vision to be preserved for future generations. Perhaps they will learn from the suffering endured by their ancestors. The reading ends on a cryptic note: "the just one, because of…faith, shall live." The Hebrew word for faith probably means faithfulness. The prophet maintains that the righteous or just one is steadfast in faithfulness, even in the midst of violence and destruction, and this faithfulness assures life.

Taken together, these readings speak to that part of us that knows we are not really self-sufficient. They assure us that we are not expected to be. Despite the remarkable abilities we may possess, we are really only limited creatures, unable to manage completely the world in which we live. The readings do not suggest that we do nothing and simply wait for God to take over, however; on the contrary, it is precisely in the face of our limitations that we must rely on God as we work to fulfill our responsibilities. Saint Augustine told us: "Pray as though everything depended on God, and work as though everything depended on you."

The prayer found in the responsorial psalm captures these sentiments. Here God is characterized as a sturdy rock and a caring shepherd, surely worthy of our confidence. We are reminded of how our religious ancestors in the wilderness failed to trust in God, despite the marvels that God was performing for them. Today is our day. Will we listen to the voice of God? Or will we too harden our hearts?

The readings demonstrate how faith is indeed "the realization of what is hoped for." In Jesus, God has already fulfilled the promises, promises that unfold as we live out our lives. Though we are often caught up in violence and destruction, we must be courageous as our lives give testimony to the faith in Christ Jesus to which we are committed. We may not live to see the tension around us resolved, but we cannot succumb to the cowardice of despair. With the help of God, faith the size of a mustard seed can uproot mighty trees, can dismantle the engines of war, and can reconcile warring parties. If we cannot accept this, it might be because we really do not have this kind of faith. Only total reliance on God and unstinting commitment to the responsibilities of life will guarantee us the blessings that God has promised.

Praying with Scripture

- Which has more influence in your life, reliance on human ingenuity and planning or reliance on God?

- Ask God to keep you faithful, especially in the midst of difficulties.

- Pray the psalm response slowly, asking God to fill you with the kind of assurance you need.

TWENTY-EIGHTH SUNDAY IN ORDINARY TIME
Readings:
2 Kgs 5:14–17; Ps 98:1–4;
2 Tim 2:8–13; Luke 17:11–19

THE BROAD EMBRACE OF GOD

We may think that leprosy, known today as Hansen's disease, is an ancient affliction, eradicated from today's society. In fact, the current World Health Organization considers it one of the major health problems in developing countries. Actually, what is called leprosy in the Bible may have been any skin ailment, from the dreaded disease to psoriasis or eczema. Such conditions were not only feared because of the possibility of contagion, but also abhorred because of the nature of their oozing sores. Besides the hygienic reason for the quarantine imposed on all those who were so afflicted, there was a religious stigma attached. Running sores kept people from participating in religious celebrations. They were thereby deemed unclean, unfit to be counted among a people who considered themselves "a kingdom of priests, a holy nation" (Exod 19:6).

The stories we hear today are more about the gratitude of the men cured than of the actual healings themselves. Naaman was not only an outcast because of his illness, but also a non-Israelite; yet he returned to Elisha to thank him for the cure, and in gratitude he transferred his allegiance to the God of Israel. This is revealed in his request for some Israelite ground so that, when he returned to his own country, he would be able to worship the God of Israel on some of the land of Israel. Similar details are found in the gospel healing account. There we are told that only the despised Samaritan returned to Jesus to give thanks for having been cured.

The nationalities of the men who were cured are not insignificant to the stories of their healings. Both the author of 2 Kings and the evangelist Luke wanted to make an important theological point about outsiders. One would presume that members of the chosen people would be grateful for God's special care of them, but one would not expect the same gratitude from nonbelievers. And yet both Naaman and the Samaritan returned to the person responsible for their cure, eager to show how grateful they were. Furthermore, Naaman shifted his allegiance to the God of Israel, and the Samaritan was extolled by Jesus for his faith.

Faith is the theme proclaimed in the reading from 2 Timothy as well. Paul was imprisoned for his faith. Still, this did not deter him from proclaiming the salvation won by Christ Jesus. He taught that this salvation reconciles us with God. This is not unlike the healing from leprosy that reincorporated the formerly afflicted men into their respective communities. Paul further insisted that the claim he made was trustworthy. At issue was whether or not those who heard this claim would accept it.

The same claim is posed to us, and, as always, it requires faith. But then it was faith that prompted Naaman to plunge himself into the waters of the Jordan River, and it was in faith that those cured went to present themselves to the priests who alone could authenticate their healing. It seems that faith and healing go hand in hand, as do faith and reconciliation. It is also clear that where there is faith, God is not outdone in generosity.

The stories of the men with leprosy have several other implications for us today. First, they demonstrate the universal love of God for all peoples. Naaman was a dignitary of a nation that often posed a threat to Israel. The Samaritan belonged to another such nation. Both nations were despised as enemies. Yet God reached out and restored these men, and in response they somehow aligned themselves with God. In neither case did the men modify their national loyalties. Israelites may have continued to consider them adversaries of the nation, but they could no longer judge them to be enemies of God.

Second, leprosy was considered one of the most, if not *the* most, loathsome of diseases. It was seen as the punishment for extraordinary sinfulness, and it rendered one ritually unclean. All righteous people shunned those afflicted with the disease, lest they too would contract the ritual impurity and be prevented from taking part in public worship. These men were healed without any admission of or repentance for sin. Thus were overturned the ritual taboo and religious shame associated with the disease. Clearly, God looks beyond human mores and strictures in order to touch the heart as well as the body.

Finally, just as these stories reveal the unconditional, universal love of God, so they show that grateful response to that love is also beyond human boundaries of race, nation, or religion. In other words, salvation unfolds in the lives of people of integrity regardless of their ethnic or religious background. Not only were the men in the accounts not enemies of God, but they were also bound to God by relationships of faith. Their relationships were different from those enjoyed by the Israelites, but they were genuine nonetheless. Once again we stand in awe before the mystery of God's love.

Praying with Scripture

- Reflect on your attitude toward people of different religious backgrounds.

- Are there groups that you shun because you consider them sinners?

- Pray for the grace to understand and appreciate God's love for all people.

TWENTY-NINTH SUNDAY IN ORDINARY TIME
Readings:
Exod 17:8–13; Ps 121:1–8;
2 Tim 3:14—4:2; Luke 18:1–8

HANG IN THERE!

We are not a patient people. We want immediate results. We depend on fast food; we are used to instant communication. This disposition is particularly obvious in the popularity of quick-weight-loss programs. Perseverance is not high on our list of cultural values. In fact, we hardly ever hear it discussed in religious circles either. This is strange, because we know that we will get nowhere in life without it. A marriage will not endure if there is no willingness to persevere in hard times. We must keep on practicing if we hope to become accomplished musicians. We will never advance in any profession or business or sport if we do not "hang in there." All the readings for today talk about perseverance. The first reading recounts an example of perseverance in prayer: Paul admonishes Timothy to persevere in proclaiming the word; the woman in the gospel exemplifies perseverance in the quest for justice. Perhaps we can find a lesson or two here.

The militant character of the reading from Exodus and the notion that God determines success in war trouble many people today. And rightly so. Since we do not share ancient Israel's perception of divine intervention in war, however, we probably do not understand their stories as they did. The point to be made here is the need for persistence in prayer, despite the hardship we might encounter in the effort.

A second feature of this story that is pertinent for us is the notion of communal support. There are times in life when we cannot do without the support of others. The burden may be ours, but we need not be alone as we bear it. What is required is humility on our part, for we will have to admit that we really cannot endure it alone. The same is true when the shoe is on the other foot. There will be times when, like Aaron and Hur, we might be called upon to support someone else. The need for perseverance in prayer and the importance of communal support are lessons we can derive from this first reading.

The woman in the gospel is not the stereotypical old shrew. She is someone who suffers threefold prejudice. As a woman in a patriarchal society, she is severely restricted. As a widow in that society, she has no male advocate and so is readily deprived of legal protection. Added to this, the judge is not rendering a just judgment. Yet she stands up bravely against the system that repeatedly discriminates against her. And she is held up as an example of one who will not capitulate in the face of opposition.

Paul, acting as a kind of mentor to Timothy, admonishes him to persevere in proclaiming the gospel. Anyone committed to such a ministry knows the struggles involved. Trying to convince people who are skeptical is not easy; having to reprimand those who have made mistakes is not pleasant; and constantly encouraging people who do not respond to it can become disheartening. Proclaiming the gospel is not always convenient.

The psalm response may have been chosen because it picks up the theme of the mountain found in the first reading. However, it actually serves as an appropriate prayer of confidence for any situation that calls for perseverance. The mountain is a metaphor for the dwelling place of God, and it is to God that we look for the help we need to persevere. God is characterized as a guardian who will keep us from harm, a place of shade where we are safe from the burning sun. Such a God will surely grant us the strength we need.

Details of each of the readings may be far from our own experience, but the messages that they hold are all relevant. We live in times of great distress. Wars, large and small, are being waged all over the world. People are often faced with a serious decision: Do they want to win the war? Or do they want to win real peace? It seems that today they can seldom achieve both, because peace requires some form of reconciliation, not merely conquest. This is a time when we must turn to God and persevere in prayer. It is a time when we must support one another in our efforts toward such commitment. The gospel story should encourage all of us who experience injustice of any kind. Like the woman who bore the burden of discrimination, we must not waver in demanding just judgments. Though not included in this passage, the notion of communal support is a theme for our consideration this Sunday. Therefore, it prompts us to ask ourselves what we do to support those who suffer discrimination.

Finally, as baptized Christians, we are all called to proclaim the gospel. We do this primarily by the character of our lives. Our honesty, our generosity, our willingness to forgive often serve to convince, reprimand, or encourage others. Paul's words can speak to all of us: "Be persistent whether it is convenient or inconvenient."

Praying with Scripture

- In what areas of your life have you genuinely matured? What values do you need to hand on to the next generation?

- What specific steps can you take to see that justice is established?

- Pray the psalm response slowly and thoughtfully.

THIRTIETH SUNDAY IN ORDINARY TIME
Readings:
Sir 35:12–14, 16–18; Ps 34:2–3, 17–19, 23;
2 Tim 4:6–8, 16–18; Luke 18:9–14

GOD, AM I GOOD!

We probably all have long lists of things we would never do. I would never rob a bank, or attack a helpless person, or run off with the pool man. It is beneath my dignity to cheat on a test or purchase clothing I intend to wear only once and then return for refund. God, am I good! But then, I have never been financially hopeless; I have never been under attack myself; and I have never had a pool man. I have never been desperate enough to feel the need to cheat or to finagle clothing. God, am I good? Or have I just been sheltered from some of the hardships that many others face? How might I act if I were in their difficult situations?

It is so easy for people who conform to acceptable patterns of behavior to sit in judgment and consider themselves better than those who do not. This is not to imply that they should disregard these standards. On the contrary, societies could not survive or thrive without their insisting on standards for living. Rather, it is to suggest that there is a difference between being righteous and being self-righteous. Truly righteous or virtuous people know that they too are capable of contemptible behavior. They know that it is only because of the goodness of God that they have been spared situations in which their weaknesses would have over-powered them. The truly righteous are fundamentally humble. The self-righteous, on the other hand, take full credit for their admirable actions. They do not consider the influence that circumstances may have on their behavior. They are proud of themselves; they boast of their adherence to moral principles; and they look down on those who unsuccessfully struggle with life in ways that they do not.

153

We would all benefit from reflecting on whether we are indeed as righteous as we claim. Are we genuinely virtuous, or have we been preserved from circumstances that might bring out the worst in us? Is our goodness tried and true, or is it simply habitual behavior expected of people like us? The challenge of Satan in the Book of Job might be directed toward any one of us: "Is it for nothing that Job is God-fearing? Have you not surrounded him and his family and all that he has with your protection?...But now put forth your hand and touch everything that he has, and surely he will blaspheme you to your face" (Job 1:10–11). In other words, take away the safeguards, and what will result?

Only those who can acknowledge their own human weaknesses feel the need to turn to God in prayer with sentiments of humility. They know that any goodness that they might exhibit is itself a gift from God. Those who stand before God and others with an attitude of "look what I have made of myself" will, however, hardly realize the need to ask for God's help in doing good. They will presume that they can manage it by themselves.

The Pharisee in the gospel very likely did live a life devoid of greed, dishonesty, and adultery. He probably did fast and tithe. But he did not realize that it was the goodness of God that lifted him up so that he could act in this righteous manner. Rather, he believed that it was his own goodness that lifted him up above sinners. On the other hand, in order to gain a livelihood, the tax collector probably extorted others. He was a sinner and he knew it. But he also knew that only God could lift him up. It was his humble demeanor that earned him God's praise.

The passage from the letter to Timothy shows that in some ways Paul resembles both the Pharisee and the tax collector. Like the Pharisee, he boasts of his accomplishments. He has competed well; he has finished the race; he has kept the faith; he has earned a crown of righteousness. Paul never denies the character of his commitment or the extent of his ministerial success. Like the tax collector, however, he knows the source of his ability to accomplish these things: "The Lord stood by me and gave me strength." According to Paul, all the glory belongs to God. Without God, Paul would have remained an enemy of the infant church.

In the body of Christ, there is no room for arrogance. We are all limited human beings with weaknesses that can trip us up if we are not vigilant. We are all poor and lowly, in need of the protection and strength that come to us from God. We are all sinners dependent on divine mercy. How foolish it is to think that we are better than others. How wrong it is to treat those others with disrespect or disdain. The last words of the gospel reading are a warning to us all. They alert us to God's propensity to turn human considerations upside down: Those who exalt themselves will be humbled; those who humble themselves will be exalted.

Praying with Scripture

- Pray for the insight to recognize how dependent you are on God for the good you are able to accomplish.

- Pray for the humility to acknowledge those areas in your life where you are controlled by your weaknesses.

- Pray for the strength to restrain those weaknesses.

THIRTY-FIRST SUNDAY IN ORDINARY TIME
Readings:
Wis 11:22—12:2; Ps 145:1-2, 8-11, 13-14;
2 Thess 1:11—2:2; Luke 19:1-10

MAKE YOURSELF AT HOME

Genuine hospitality is a social art. It might also be characterized as an intricate dance. Everyone involved must know the steps, but they also have to be able to feel the rhythm of the others. They have to know when to move forward, how far to go; they have to know when to step back, and to what extent. And they have to know how fast to move. The hospitable host generously offers the warmth and comfort of a home; the grateful guest humbly accepts the offer. If either one acts with too much speed or too slowly, they could end up stepping on each other's toes. Being invited to someone's home is also a sign of one's standing in the community. After all, we don't all get invitations to the White House, and few of us host celebrities or dignitaries.

In several ways the gospel story redefines the ancient protocol of hospitality. Whether he was an honest man or not, as the chief tax collector, Zacchaeus earned his living by working for the occupying Romans. Tax collectors were not salaried. They simply added their own living expenses to the taxes levied by the Romans. The story says that he was wealthy. This means that he must have prospered at the expense of others. It is easy to see why his occupation made him unacceptable in the eyes of many. No self-respecting Jew would think of being a guest in the home of such a sinner. This does not bother Jesus. In fact, he disregards the protocol of hospitality and invites himself to Zacchaeus's home. He is leading in the dance, and he is changing the steps as he goes along.

This story has delightful twists. We have a man of significant social and economic stature, who is also slight in physical stature. When he hears that Jesus is passing through town, he puts aside all decorum and, like a child, he climbs into a tree so that he can see. Not only does he see, but he is also seen. Zacchaeus knows that Jesus is more than a guest, for he promises him that he would make amends for any dishonesty of which he might be guilty. In fact, he goes to extremes in this. On the surface, this is an account about hospitality, and Zacchaeus the host should lead in the dance. A closer look shows that this is really an offer of salvation, and in such circumstances the initiative is always God's. So, Jesus offers salvation; Zacchaeus then offers hospitality; Jesus accepts hospitality; and Zacchaeus accepts salvation.

God's willingness to reach out to the sinner is also seen in the reading from Wisdom. The author first maintains that the immensity of the entire universe is minuscule when compared with the magnificence of the Creator. Furthermore, it is this Creator who shows mercy toward sinners. And why does God show mercy? "For you love all things that are / and loathe nothing that you have made; / for what you hated, you would not have fashioned." God loves all creation because God made it. Similarly, one might say that God made all creation because God loves it.

The author of Wisdom then moves from natural creation generally to human beings, referring to God as the "lover of souls." This is not the passion associated with *éros*, or the friendship identified as *philía*, but the wholehearted commitment of *agápe*. God's mercy flows from this kind of love. The technical covenant words *graciousness*, *mercy*, and *compassion*, found in the psalm, describe the sentiments that prompt God to call all of us to salvation and invite us to make ourselves at home there.

The gospel first appears as a story of social hospitality, but it soon becomes clear that the hospitality presented to us for our consideration is divine, not human. It consists of the grace of salvation, not the comforts of physical satisfaction. The passage from 2 Thessalonians offers us another picture of salvation. Like Jesus before him, Paul is concerned with the spiritual well-being of others. He has preached the message of salvation to them. He now prays that it will take root in their minds and hearts. He prays that they will be steadfast in their commitment, even if the fulfillment of their hopes does not appear on the horizon. He knows that the first excitement of conversion can soon wear thin. (We have no idea if Zacchaeus's enthusiasm was long lasting.) But Paul was convinced that the openness or hospitality of God endures forever.

In the ancient world, the protocol of hospitality was practiced by all peoples. Today, Western cultures are more individualistic. Unfortunately, we do not always feel responsible for the well-being of others. Consequently, Christian hospitality is somewhat countercultural. Still, it is an attitude of mind and heart to which we all are called. We must remember that God is the lover of all souls. We see divine openness in Jesus, who reached out to all, even those considered by society to be unworthy.

Praying with Scripture

- Go out of your way to be open and kind to someone who is not part of your social or religious circle.

- Follow the example of Zacchaeus and make amends where you might have taken advantage of someone.

- Pray the responsorial psalm slowly, reflecting on God's gracious kindness in your life.

THIRTY-SECOND SUNDAY IN ORDINARY TIME
Readings:
Macc 7:1–2, 9–14; Ps 17:1, 5–6, 8, 15;
2 Thess 2:16—3:5; Luke 20:27–38

WHAT HAPPENS NEXT?

There is within every living being an innate tendency to cling to life and to flourish. It is no different with human beings. In fact, it is this passion for life that often causes us anxiety in the face of death. The value that various peoples ascribe to the human spirit can be seen in the practices with which they surround death. Some cultures return the body to the earth or the sea from which they believe it came. Others lift it up into the heavens. Burial grounds are always considered sacred places. But what about death itself? Is it the end? If not, what happens next? These are questions that have occupied thinking people from time immemorial. The inevitability of death makes them puzzle over the meaning of life. The readings for today are evidence of a change from ancient Israel's understanding of the possibility of life after this life.

The early Israelites did not have a clear idea of life after death. They believed that the dead went to a shadowy underworld known as Sheol, which was a place of neither reward nor punishment. Unlike the Greeks who came later, the Israelites had no concept of an immortal soul. Furthermore, they believed that their God was a God of the living, not of the dead. While other nations venerated gods of the underworld, Israel did not. Still, they did not think that death resulted in total annihilation.

The first reading from 2 Maccabees reflects the time when Israel was under the influence of Greek conquerors who were trying to force devout Jews to renounce their religious practices. While the scene lays bare the horror of persecution, it also describes the valor of those being tortured. It reveals something else as well. Three of the brothers speak, and each of them finds strength in the belief that they will eventually be raised up by God. There is no mention here of an immortal soul; focus is on the resurrection of the dead. This is one of the earliest biblical references to some form of existence after this life.

The same theme of the resurrection of the dead is the basis of the confrontation described in the gospel passage. The Sadducees, who did not believe in the resurrection of the dead, use an ancient marriage practice in an attempt to make a mockery of the belief. Jesus refutes them by insisting that in the age of the resurrection there will be no need to further the human race through procreation, because there will be no death. He also states the traditional belief that God is the God of the living.

There is a difference between the way Jesus understands the notion of God as God of the living and not the dead and the way it was understood by the ancient Israelites. Originally, the reference was to those who were actually alive. With this new concept of resurrection, those who have died and been raised from the dead are considered living in a new way. In other words, "all are alive"—both the living and the dead who have been raised.

The question can be posed again: What happens next? Neither of the readings really answers that question, but they do assure us that there is something that will happen next. This is not a demonstrable fact, however; it is a statement of faith. And from where does faith in the resurrection of the dead originate? Clearly, it is not from the Greek notion of an immortal soul, but from trust in God. This trust is grounded in a theme that is implicit in the theology of Israel, though not explicitly mentioned in today's readings. That theme is covenant.

The brothers who appear in the first reading are clearly devout Jews, faithful to their covenant obligations. The Sadducees in the gospel appeal to the teaching of Moses, evidence that both they and their hearers belong to the people of God. Jesus calls the dead "children of God." A covenant relationship is presumed. The bonds of covenant are the basis of the trust in God evident in these readings. Because of this trust, Israel did not ever seem willing to concede that these bonds were severed at death. Christian theology was very clear about this point as well: "For I am convinced that neither death, nor life...will be able to separate us from the love of God in Christ Jesus our Lord" (Rom 8:38–39).

Following in the footsteps of our religious ancestors, we too trust that the bonds of love that join us with God are indestructible. Since it was God who invited us into this covenant relationship, surely God will see that this bond endures through death and beyond, whatever that beyond might hold. Here too we can only trust in God, for we have no idea of what lies ahead of us. As we read elsewhere: "We are God's children now; what we shall be has not yet been revealed" (1 John 3:2).

Praying with Scripture

- What do you do to strengthen the covenant bonds that join you to God?

- Pray for the courage to remain steadfast in your faith regardless of the price you may have to pay.

- Commit yourself to the love of God so that you will be able to face peacefully the inevitability of your own death.

THIRTY-THIRD SUNDAY IN ORDINARY TIME
Readings:
Mal 3:19–20a; Ps 98:5–9;
2 Thess 3:7–12; Luke 21:5–19

THE END OF DAYS

There is always a great deal of emotion in anticipation of "the day," whether that be a wedding day, the first day of vacation, opening day at the ball park, or the day of discharge from the service, to name but a few important days in the lives of many of us. In cases such as these, not only is the day enjoyed for itself, but it also promises many more wonderful days in the future. On the other hand, there are some days that strike fear and dread in our hearts, such as the day we lose our job, the day of the death of a loved one, the day we are sent out to fight a war. These days thrust us into sadness and struggle with little or no light at the end of the tunnel.

The "day of the LORD" was always a day of anticipation for the people of ancient Israel. Originally it was perceived as a day of fulfillment. It was the moment in history when all of the promises made by God would come to completion and the people of God would enjoy them forever, promises of peace and prosperity, of contentment and harmony. Many of the prophets looked forward to that day and described it in terms that remind us of the garden of Eden before Adam and Eve had sinned and been driven out. Jesus claimed that this long-awaited day was dawning as he inaugurated the reign of God, but the sinfulness of the people required that there be a period of purging before that fulfillment could come to pass. For this reason, some of the prophets warned that the "day of the LORD" would first be a day of suffering. They even compared that suffering to the pangs that preceded birth, a symbol of new life coming out of suffering. In fact, such suffering was sometimes referred to as the birth pangs of the Messiah. Today's readings focus on the painful aspects of "that day."

The prophet Malachi shows us both dimensions of that future day. For the sinful, it will be a day of fiery purification; for the righteous, it will be a day of healing. The gospel reading is quite explicit about the suffering that will take place. The description found there may have originally been written to exhort the persecuted Christians to remain faithful regardless of the cost. They were encouraged to perceive their very real distress as the purification that would precede the coming of the final age of fulfillment.

Like all of the Bible's depictions of the future, these descriptions are symbolic in nature. They are meant to inspire believers to derive whatever good they can from life's inevitable suffering. Contrary to what some people might think, they do not point to specific historical occurrences; they are not blueprints of the events taking place in our own world. Rather, they are goads meant to spur us on with steadfastness. "By your perseverance you will secure your lives."

The early Christians believed that after Jesus' resurrection and ascension he would return and bring all things to completion. It seems that some felt that since the day of fulfillment had already dawned with the coming of Jesus, all they had to do was wait for his return. It is this attitude that Paul criticized. He placed himself before the Thessalonians as an example to follow. He worked hard and was a burden to no one. So should they all work, and if any refused to do so, they should not be allowed to live off the community, "neither should that one eat." In other words, Christians must assume their fair share of responsibility in this world as they await the final dawning of the time of fulfillment.

Today's readings reflect the suffering side of our faith, a faith that claims that God can bring life out of death. It also insists that the age of fulfillment, which is the age of new life, will not dawn until we are purified of our sinfulness. Thus, life's inescapable suffering, if accepted and endured in the spirit of Jesus, can act as a purifying agent. Today the challenge of acceptance and endurance is placed before us.

It is appropriate that we consider the advent of this age of fulfillment as the liturgical year comes to a close. During the year, we have been led through the mysteries of death and resurrection, and now the drama of our faith is about to be brought to fulfillment. Today's psalm response reminds us just how this drama will end: "The LORD.../ comes to rule the earth; / he will rule the world with justice / and the peoples with equity." Thus, though the readings focus on the suffering of "that day," we are reminded that the final scene is one of victory and fulfillment. And lo, that day is surely coming.

Praying with Scripture

- Pray that the inevitable sufferings of life may make you a better person, not a bitter one.

- Pray the psalm response, remembering that ultimately Christ triumphs over suffering and death.

- In what ways do you help build up the community?

CHRIST THE KING
Readings:
2 Sam 5:1–3; Ps 122:1–5;
Col 1:12–20; Luke 23:35–43

LONG LIVE THE KING!

Probably the best-known royal leader in the world today is Queen Elizabeth II of England. Although her leadership role is in many ways more ceremonial than administrative, her official title is still quite impressive. She is Queen Elizabeth II by the grace of God, queen of this realm and of her other realms and territories, head of the commonwealth, defender of the faith.

Today we celebrate the feast of Christ the King, a feast established by Pope Pius XI in 1925 because the people of the day had "thrust Jesus Christ and his holy law out of their lives" and "these had no place in public affairs or in politics." The pope went on to claim "that as long as individuals and states refused to submit to the rule of our Savior, there would be no really hopeful prospect of a lasting peace among nations." This critique of the situation of the world could have been written today, more than eighty years later. One has to wonder how believing people could have failed so miserably to make a change in the world. Have we really accepted Christ as our king?

Just how did the carpenter from Nazareth come to be regarded as a king? During his public life the title "King of the Jews" belonged to Herod, the puppet king set up by the Roman occupiers (Luke 23:6–12). Nowhere in the gospels does Jesus claim this title for himself. In fact, it was used to mock him while he was hanging on the cross. It was probably several years after his resurrection that Christians began to apply that title to him. But why?

One of the tasks of the early Christian teachers was to show that Jesus was indeed the fulfillment of the religious expectations of the Jewish people. They did this by placing him squarely at the heart of some of Israel's major religious traditions. By means of a genealogy, his ancestry can be traced back to David, the one regarded as the ideal king. Today's first reading reminds us of this. Since the ancient king was thought to be the shepherd or protector of the people and the commander of its forces, these characterizations would also be passed on to the rightful heir of this royal tradition. Thus we can say that Jesus is king by the grace of God, shepherd of the people and commander of Israel.

In the gospel we see that some of the rulers, the soldiers, and even one of the criminals crucified with Jesus threw royal titles in his face. If he was the chosen one, "the Christ of God...the King of the Jews," he should have been able to save himself. In response to such taunts, Jesus promised salvation to the criminal who did recognize his royal nature and who thus cried out: "Remember me when you come into your kingdom." Jesus' response, "Today you will be with me in Paradise," shows that Jesus is indeed a king, though he reigns from a bloody cross rather than from a majestic throne.

When we turn to the Letter to the Colossians we find that Paul adds several divine appellations to Jesus' royal title. He is God's beloved Son, the image of the invisible God, the firstborn of all creation. What do these titles tell us about our king? First and foremost, they tell us that, as God's beloved Son, our king has direct and immediate access to God. He does not have to work through any parliament or congress. In the ancient world, an image of a god was set up to indicate where that God exercised a sovereign rule. As image of the invisible God, Jesus marks where God rules. In other words, our king is the symbol of divine sovereignty. Finally, as the firstborn of creation, he is the promise of all the good things that will follow.

One further set of appellations characterizes Christ as our king. Just as the previously mentioned titles flow from his union with God, these mark his relationship with us. As Risen Lord he is the head of the church and the firstborn of the dead. As head of the church, he is intimately joined to us his members. As firstborn from the dead, he is the promise of our own resurrection. If we were to bring together all of the honorific titles found in today's readings, the listing would be unparalleled in the annals of royalty.

Jesus is king by the grace of God, shepherd of the people and commander of Israel, God's beloved Son, the image of the invisible God, the firstborn of all creation, head of the church, and first-born of the dead. Despite such honors ascribed to him, "as individuals and as states [we have] refused to submit to the rule of our Savior." This last Sunday of the liturgical year we are given an opportunity to recommit ourselves to him, for we know so well that without him there can be "no really hopeful prospect of a lasting peace among nations."

Praying with Scripture

- Renew the baptismal promises that commit you to the reign of God.

- Which of Christ's titles makes the most difference in your life? Why?

- What can you do this week to bring Christ's reign into the life of another?

Solemnities and Feasts

TRINITY (SOLEMNITY)
Readings:
Prov 8:22–31; Ps 8:4–9;
Rom 5:1–5; John 16:12–15

I BELIEVE IN GOD

Legend tells us that St. Patrick used the three-leafed clover to teach his people about the three persons in one God. It is an ingenious pedagogical device, very neat and understandable—but it does little to explain the mystery we call God. Nor do the readings for this feast explain either the divine essence or how the three persons of the Trinity interact with one another. They employ the language of Father, Son, and Holy Spirit without explaining that these titles describe the inner relationships among the three persons of the Trinity, not their relationships with us. The readings do throw some light, however, on ways in which the Triune God touches our lives. Relating this activity with three statements found in the Apostles' Creed will demonstrate this.

"I believe in God the Father almighty, creator of heaven and earth." In the first reading from Proverbs we hear primordial wisdom, the only witness to God's creative activity, describe the ease and artistry with which the Almighty fashioned our universe. The splendor of creation is but a reflection of the magnificence of the wondrous Creator. The threatening chaotic waters of the deep were no match for this divine architect, who simply established the vault of the heavens above them. The unruly sea was also secured within land boundaries, making the land safe for its inhabitants. Not only is the structure of the natural world mysterious and breathtaking, but it is also reliable. Its orderly arrangement allows all creatures to follow their natural paths.

For our part, all we need to do is look around to behold the expanse of the sky that covers us and delights us with its ever-changing display of light and color, or stand in amazement at the generosity of the earth that feeds us with such liberality. The natural world is a canvas upon which is painted awesome beauty that enriches our minds and hearts; it is a storehouse of nourishment and delight that sustains our bodies and our spirits. And this all comes to us from the hand of a loving Creator.

"...and in Jesus Christ, [God's] only son, our Lord." In all of his writings, Paul, the great christological teacher, insists that it is Jesus who saves us. In today's reading from the Letter to the Romans, he further explains how each person of the Trinity plays a role in our salvation. This salvation begins with faith in Jesus. It is this faith that justifies us and establishes peace with God. This new relationship of peace is the basis of our hope. Furthermore, Paul declares that "the love of God has been poured into our hearts through the Holy Spirit." In this short reading we discover the possible relationship binding affliction, endurance, character, and hope. In this way we see how faith, hope, and love flow together and are the ground of our Christian living.

The faith that Paul tells us is salvific is a living faith. It calls us to believe firmly that we have been born anew through our baptism into the death and resurrection of Jesus. This means that we now live according to the teachings of Jesus, patterning our lives after his. This faith calls us to live lives of hope, confident that the battle against evil has already been fought and won, and that through our manner of Christian living it will become apparent to others. This faith calls us to genuine love of others, as Jesus loves them. The salvation of which Paul speaks is grounded in the love of God in which we live.

"I believe in the Holy Spirit." In the gospel account for today, Jesus refers to this Spirit as the Spirit of truth. As in the passage from Paul, here too all three divine persons work in our lives. Jesus says that his Father has given all things to him; Jesus himself teaches us truths that we will not yet be able to understand; finally, it is the Spirit who glorifies Jesus and guides us in our search for the truth of Jesus' teaching. We might say that Jesus teaches us what the Father wants us to know so that we can live lives of integrity. Because this teaching is too deep for us to comprehend, we need the Spirit to bring us to an understanding of it.

It is not enough to profess our faith in the Triune God: We must live as if we truly believe what we proclaim. Today's readings help us to realize that we have been saved by our Triune God and are continually brought by this same God to a deeper appreciation of the truths of a life of faith. That life is one to be lived in union with God and with one another. The unity within the Trinity is the model placed before us today. The three divine persons work together for the salvation of all. So too must we work together for the good of all.

Praying with Scripture

- Spend some time today luxuriating in the beauty of the natural world, and give thanks to the Creator for such marvelous gifts.

- How have the death and resurrection of Jesus made a difference in your life?

- Pray that the Holy Spirit might enlighten you to see more clearly the goodness of God.

THE MOST PRECIOUS BODY AND BLOOD OF CHRIST (SOLEMNITY)

Readings:
*Gen 14:18–20; Ps 110:1–4;
1 Cor 11:23–26; Luke 9:11b–17*

ALL YOU CAN EAT!

The feast of the Most Precious Body and Blood of Christ combines what were previously two separate celebrations. Originally, each feast concentrated on one aspect of the awesome mystery of the Eucharist, Christ's body or his blood. Joined together, they better illumine the depth and richness of this theology. Looking at important themes of first the Sacred Body and then the Precious Blood will help us to appreciate the richness of what is now celebrated as one feast.

The Sacred Body: Before we realized that our obsession with food and the widespread habit of overindulging ourselves would result in a national epidemic of obesity, many people flocked to restaurants that advertised "supersize" or "all you can eat!" In order to keep pace with our demand for more food, restaurants served portions that were often twice the amount the average person should consume at one sitting. The line between "eat to live" and "live to eat" seems to have become blurred. We are now paying dearly to take off the weight that over the years we have put on.

The feast we celebrate today puts a very different spin on the phrase "all you can eat!" Both the reading from Genesis and the responsorial psalm mention Melchizedek, the ancient king who was also a priest. Though originally this mysterious figure exemplified the superior nature of the establishment in Jerusalem, in Christian theology Melchizedek and his offering prefigure Jesus and his offering. Though Melchizedek's offering should not be seen as eucharistic in the sacramental sense of the word, it was an act of thanksgiving, for the Greek word for thanksgiving is *eucharistía*. Melchizedek offered bread and wine, the staples of life, and the bread that Jesus offers us can certainly be considered the staple of life.

The never-ending supply of bread with which Jesus fed the multitude prefigured his own body, the consecrated bread that sustains us until he will come again. The gospel account itself makes this connection, for there we read words that are also found in the eucharistic rite: "He said the blessing over them, broke them, and gave them [to eat]" (Luke 9:16); "after he had given thanks, broke it and said, 'This is my body that is for you'" (1 Cor 11:26). Today Jesus feeds us with bread that is more than mere bread; it is his very body. Furthermore, in his own prodigality he continues to invite us to eat for as long as we continue our faith journey on this earth.

The Precious Blood: Several years ago, a man entered a Benedictine monastery located in a quiet corner of the Missouri countryside. Without warning, he shot four of the monks, killing two of them before he turned the gun on himself, taking his own life. No one has yet discovered why this man acted in such a violent manner. True to the paschal mystery to which the monks had committed themselves, however, new life has sprung from this tragically spilled blood. Since that heartrending event, the community has attracted several young, vibrant men. Though they will never replace the men who were killed, they will continue the noble tradition of prayer, service, and forgiveness for which this monastery is so well-known.

The ancients believed that life is in the blood. Since all life comes from and remains in the hands of God, lifeblood itself was thought to be God's to give or to take away. Consequently, the only time one was legitimately allowed to spill blood was while offering a substitutionary sacrifice. The blood of the sacrificed animal became a stand-in for human lifeblood; the sacrificial act symbolized the offering of the life-force within humans. In line with this practice and the meaning associated with it, Jesus offered his own lifeblood as a substitute for the lifeblood of us all. As we read in Paul's First Letter to the Corinthians, Jesus' blood sealed the covenant made between God and humankind, and thus it brought new life to the world.

Many people today might be repelled by the idea of eating someone's body and drinking his blood, unless they realize the fundamental symbolism involved. Actually, in the Eucharist we eat bread that is Jesus' body and we drink wine that is his blood. This brings us back to the account of Melchizedek's sacrifice that came to stand for a reality much deeper than the actual sacrifice itself. So it is with the Eucharist. What we see and taste as bread and wine constitute a reality much deeper than the simple elements themselves.

On this feast, we celebrate our covenant with God, established through the shedding of Jesus' blood, and through his willingness to feed us with the only bread that will stave our hunger. We renew this covenant each time we participate in the banquet of his body and blood, a banquet, which, through his death, gives us life. The efficaciousness of this consecrated bread and wine is extolled again and again in the rich metaphors of the sequence for this feast. They continue to remind us that by participating in this banquet, we "proclaim the death of the Lord until he comes."

Praying with Scripture

- Reflect on your own manner of participation in the Eucharist. Spend some time thanking God for this bountiful banquet.

- In what ways has the Eucharist brought forth new life in you?

- How might you make every meal somehow eucharistic?

PRESENTATION OF THE LORD (FEAST)
Readings:
Mal 3:1–4; Ps 24:7–10;
Heb 2:14–18; Luke 2:22–40

FULFILLING THE PRESCRIPTIONS OF THE LAW

Looking back on my childhood, I realize that my parents' Catholic identity was in large part based on religious devotions. During Mass, my mother would say the rosary. There were devotions to Our Lady of Perpetual Help every Tuesday at 7:30 p.m., and Friday evenings in Lent featured the Stations of the Cross. Once a year a visiting priest came to conduct the Forty Hours' Devotion with exposition of the Blessed Sacrament followed by Benediction. By and large, several of these religious practices decreased in popularity or actually came to an end with the Second Vatican Council. Sunday liturgy became much more participative and the celebration of the Holy Week Triduum came to be seen as the high point of the liturgical year. Though some ethnic groups have preserved their own religious practices, the old practices are gone and very little has grown up in place of the very familiar devotions of the past. This is unfortunate, for such devotions brought some form of pious observance into the daily lives of people, making Catholic life more than merely a Sunday or Holy Day obligation. As unliturgical as it may have been, until the day she died, my mother still prayed the rosary during Mass.

The feast we celebrate today commemorates two religious practices of ancient Israel, namely, the purification of a woman after childbirth and the presentation of the firstborn male child. Though linked to each other, these observances were quite different. The purification of a woman who has just given birth grew out of the belief that the life-power within blood was sacred and belonged to God. Because of the mysterious nature of the power of blood, one was forbidden to touch it. Since the proper place for blood was within the body, any type of shedding of blood rendered one ritually unclean and in need of some form of purification. This explains why a woman's menstrual cycle and the birth of a child prevented her from participating in the ordinary pursuits of life. Since she bled but did not die, at such times she was actually considered possessed of power that needed to be contained. This explains why the birth of a child was surrounded with many purification regulations. It was not the birth itself that possessed the power, for the child was not considered ritually unclean. It was the blood of the mother that had to be somehow reinstated in its proper place.

We read in Leviticus:

> When a woman has conceived and gives birth to a boy, she shall be unclean for seven days, with the same uncleanness as at her menstrual period. On the eighth day, the flesh of the boy's foreskin shall be circumcised, and then she shall spend thirty-three days more in becoming purified of her blood; she shall not touch anything sacred nor enter the sanctuary till the days of her purification are fulfilled....When the days of her purification for a son...are fulfilled, she shall bring to the priest at the entrance of the meeting tent a...pigeon or a turtle dove for a sin offering. (12:2–4, 6)

Our liturgical calendar follows the sequence of these prescriptions. Eight days after Christmas we commemorate the circumcision of Jesus. Today, forty days after Christmas, we commemorate the end of Mary's purification and the presentation of the child in the Temple.

The second ritual requirement mentioned in the text was a way of reclaiming the firstborn male child who, the Israelites believed, really belonged to God. Buying back the child was a way of acknowledging God's initial claim. The standard offering for this religious practice was a yearling lamb, but provisions were made for those couples that might not be able to afford such an animal. As the gospel indicates, Mary and Joseph brought either a pair of pigeons or a pair of turtledoves.

We might think that these religious practices are quite primitive. Some women are even offended by the requirement of Mary's purification. They think that unclean means unworthy. But it doesn't. It means possessing power that is out of the ordinary, and one does not mix that mysterious power with the mysterious power that is unleashed during a religious sacrifice. Just as the rosary reminded us of the mysteries of our faith, the devotions to Our Lady of Perpetual Help were a way of pleading our cause through Mary, the Stations of the Cross enabled us to participate in Jesus' painful journey to the cross, and Forty Hours brought us into the sacramental presence of Christ, so Mary's purification acknowledged God's sovereignty over the power of life, and the presentation of Jesus acknowledged God's initial claim of every male child born.

In many ways the lack of meaningful devotions leaves our religious lives somewhat impoverished. This might explain why many of the former devotions are being reinstated, often with new meaning. For example, some parishes regularly celebrate Benediction, and to the Joyful, Sorrowful, and Glorious mysteries of the rosary, Pope John Paul II added the five Luminous mysteries. If long-standing religious practices are not enlivened or if new devotions are not given birth, we should not wonder why people search elsewhere for nourishment for their spirits.

Praying with Scripture

- In what ways do you bring the mysteries of our faith into your everyday life?

- How accepting are you of the devotional life of others?
- Do you have favorite prayers? Do you pray them often?

NATIVITY OF ST. JOHN THE BAPTIST (SOLEMNITY)
Readings:
Isa 49:1–6; Ps 139:1–3, 13–15;
Acts 13:22–26; Luke 1:57–66, 80

"WHAT, THEN, WILL THIS CHILD BE?"

It takes a big person to be content being known as someone else's daughter or son, sister or brother, or even cousin. We all want our own personal identity, not one that is dependent on the celebrity of another. Yet this is precisely how we remember John the Baptist. He was the cousin of Jesus. Historically, John did have a life of his own, one that he had carved out for himself. He was an ascetic (Matt 3:4), a not uncommon style of life for first-century Jews who were zealous in their religious observance. The gospels tell us that he had a large following (Mark 1:5), as well as some intimate disciples (John 1:35). His was not a feel-good message, as we find is the case with many popular preachers today. He challenged the people and called them to repentance. Yet it was not really this message that placed his life in jeopardy. Rather, it was his denunciation of the scandalous love affair of Herod, the ruling king of the Jews at the time. When Jesus appeared on the scene, however, John stepped out of the limelight, content to have prepared for something and someone greater than he.

It is unusual that the anniversary of someone's day of birth, someone other than Jesus, that is, would be celebrated as a solemnity. Not even Mary's birthday (September 8) has been given that honor. Yet the Nativity of John the Baptist is just such a feast. And why is this? Probably not because of what John accomplished in his own right, but because of what he represented. He announced the imminent advent of the eschatological age. Thus, he represented the end of the time of expectation and the dawning of the age of fulfillment. John was a road sign, an arrow that directed people away from him and what he represented toward another. This may appear to some to be a rather unfulfilling life work, but that was certainly not the case. When speaking of John, Jesus declared: "Among those born of women, there has been none greater than John the Baptist" (Matt 11:11).

As we learn from the gospels, everything about John's conception and birth indicated that this was an unusual child, one who had been chosen by God. An angel announced his conception, and he was born from a barren womb, of parents advanced in years (Luke 1:7, 11). Skepticism at the thought of such a birth resulted in his father's being deprived of his ability to speak during the entire time of Elizabeth's pregnancy. But Zechariah's tongue was loosened when, at the birth of the child, he insisted that the boy be given the name John, the very name told him by the angel at the time of the conception. Was John chosen because he was somehow related to Jesus? Certainly not, because the community that Jesus established was not dependent on blood relationships: "My mother and my brothers are those who hear the word of God and act on it" (Luke 8:21).

In tracing the ancestry of Jesus, the author of Acts of the Apostles included John, not because of his kinship with Jesus, but because of his role in God's plan of salvation. John was the precursor. Who originated that perception of John? It certainly was well established in the early Christian community by the time of the writing of Acts. Did the Christians get this notion from Jesus? Or did it originate with John himself? If messianic expectation was widespread in the Jewish community at this time—and it was, and John saw himself as one who was sent to call the people to reform their lives in preparation for the fulfillment of that expectation, and he seems to have done just that—then one can safely conclude that John saw himself as a precursor of the age of fulfillment. To what extent he understood Jesus' role in the unfolding of that fulfillment is another question. But he did not have to understand. All he had to do was herald the imminent coming and step back at its approach.

The Servant Songs of Isaiah, of which today's first reading is one, are usually associated with Jesus. Here, however, it is linked with John the Baptist because the phrase "The LORD called me from birth, / from my mother's womb he gave me my name" corresponds to features found in the narrative of the nativity of John. Though John was not the servant, other aspects of this reading could easily apply to him. His message of repentance certainly made him a "sharp-edged sword"; through this message he did seek to "raise up the tribes of Jacob, / and restore the survivors of Israel."

Though our birth may not have been announced by an angel, it was nonetheless an important event in God's overall plan of salvation, for we too have been chosen to be heralds of the good news. John announced the coming of the age of fulfillment and urged his hearers to repent in preparation for it; we proclaim that it has indeed already come, and we are privileged to be able to live within it. How faithful are we to this calling?

Praying with Scripture

- To what extent are you able to lose yourself in a cause that is bigger than you?

- We are now living in the age of fulfillment. What in your life gives witness to this profound truth?

- What in your life must you change so that you can enter into the fullness of the reign of God?

SAINTS PETER AND PAUL (SOLEMNITY)
Readings:
Acts 12:1–11; Ps 34:2–9;
2 Tim 4:6–8, 17–18; Matt 16:13–19

PILLARS OF THE CHURCH

When I was growing up, my mother belonged to that amorphous group of people known as the "pillars of the church." They were those members one would always find working around the church. She did not play the organ and conduct the choir or take care of the sanctuary or wash the altar linen, as some of the women did, but she could always be called on to help with the cooking when there was a breakfast or a dinner or a meal after a funeral. This was all volunteer work, but it was essential if the parish was to be some form of social community.

Today we celebrate the feast of Saints Peter and Paul, two of the original pillars of the church. The readings selected for this feast throw light on why we might refer to them in this way. The gospel passage is quite straightforward. In it we hear Jesus telling Peter: "You are Peter, and upon this rock I will build my church." The choice of the metaphor *rock* has nothing to do with the stability of Peter himself, for this is the apostle who, in Jesus' darkest hour, will deny even knowing him. Rather, there is a play on the Greek words Peter (*Pétros*) and rock (*pétra*). With the exception of the statement "You *are* Peter," all of the verbs found in Jesus' declaration are a form of the future. Jesus *will* build the church; the gates of the netherworld *shall* not prevail against that church; Jesus *will* give Peter the keys of the kingdom of heaven; whatever Peter binds *shall* be bound in heaven; whatever he looses *shall* be loosed in heaven. Perhaps in that same future, Peter *will* indeed be a rock for everyone else.

The first reading from Acts of the Apostles describes an event in the life of Peter. Herod, the one who ruled at the time as king of the Jews, imprisoned Peter because of his preaching about Jesus. This episode occurred long after Peter had repented of his denial of Jesus and after his reconciliation with Jesus on the shore of the lake after the resurrection. In other words, now Peter is well aware of his own frailty and his dependence on God for both courage and strength. This reading recounts how Peter was miraculously released from prison by an angel of the Lord and reunited with the fledgling Christian community. Peter can now be a rock for them because he knows the source of his stability.

The other pillar of the church is Paul. Writing to Timothy, one of his own close disciples, Paul shows himself to be a mature Christian, seasoned by the realities of the ministry. His own self-evaluation is quite complimentary: "I have competed well; I have finished the race; I have kept the faith." This is not the bragging of a proud man. Paul has indeed been a faithful disciple of Jesus and a successful herald of the gospel, but he is not slow to admit the source of his effectiveness: "The Lord stood by me and gave me strength."

Though he was appointed by Jesus to be the leader among all of the disciples, in the earliest days of the Christian community Peter was very closely associated with the Jewish-Christian community in Jerusalem. It was Peter who stood up and courageously preached the first sermon to the crowds who had come to Jerusalem to celebrate the Jewish feast of Pentecost (Acts 2:14–36); it was Peter who addressed the people in the Temple after a crippled beggar had been cured; it was Peter who fearlessly spoke to the Jewish leaders in the Sanhedrin; it was Peter who accepted into the church the first Gentiles, the centurion Cornelius and his household. Peter is the principal character in most of the stories found in the first thirteen chapters of Acts of the Apostles.

The story of the growth of the church changes in chapter thirteen of Acts. At that time, Paul appears as the prominent preacher. He is the one who takes the message of the gospel out into the broader Mediterranean world. Though initially Paul and his companions go first to the Jews who gather in the synagogues for prayer and teaching, they soon turn to the Gentile communities of the world. Just as Peter is the apostle to the Jews, Paul is the apostle to the Gentiles. These two titles suggest that all peoples were evangelized.

By the grace of God, these weak men became true pillars of the church. We are the proof of their effectiveness. The future of the church is now in our hands. Today we are being asked to do more than provide food for parish celebrations. We are being summoned to proclaim the gospel in our homes and in our places of work, to live lives of integrity courageously and confidently, knowing that God's grace is no less available to us than it was to Peter and Paul before us.

Praying with Scripture

- In what ways might you be more involved in the life of your local parish?

- Pray to St. Peter that you might be open to the ways in which God is calling you to give witness to the people in your life.

- Pray to St. Paul that you might be open to people of other faith traditions.

TRANSFIGURATION OF THE LORD (FEAST)
Readings:
Dan 7:9–10, 13–14; Ps 97:1–2, 5–6, 9;
2 Pet 1:16–19; Luke 9:28b–36

YOU'VE GOT TO BE KIDDING!

"You've got to be kidding!" That is a phrase we often use to express our astonishment that someone would think that we could be hoodwinked into believing the unbelievable or trying to do the impossible. It is a way of saying: "Do you think I'm stupid? Give me a break!" No one wants to appear gullible. That is for children or for the very unsophisticated, not for those of us who are worldly wise.

Today's gospel reading ends by telling us that Peter, John, and James, the three apostles who had witnessed Jesus' transfiguration and heard the voice from heaven, "did not at that time tell anyone what they has seen." Who would have believed them even if they had done so? What they had witnessed was so incredible that even the other apostles might have questioned their claims and responded: "You've got to be kidding!" True, they had already seen Jesus cast out demons and heal the sick, but to have him transformed before their very eyes and to see him conversing with Moses and Elijah, the two greatest figures from their religious past, was more than they could comprehend. But then, that might have been precisely their error. They might have presumed that eventually they would be able to comprehend Jesus.

Today's readings are filled with features that are impossible to comprehend. The gospel and the reading from 2 Peter call our attention to details found in the account of the event of the transfiguration itself. They both speak of the blinding majesty of Jesus that shone forth from him, a majesty that originated from God. This was the man with whom the apostles had been spending all of their time. They knew the contours of his face, the way his eyes expressed what was on his mind. His manner of dress was no different from theirs. Now, without warning, "his face changed in appearance and his clothing became dazzling white." They had no explanation for this. The two readings also repeat the words that were heard from the cloud, referring to Jesus as God's own Son. This must certainly have shaken the three men. Being Galileans themselves, they probably knew Jesus' natural family. Now a voice from heaven says: "This is my chosen Son." They had no explanation for this either.

It is not that the disciples did not know their religious tradition. They must have been somewhat familiar with the passage from the Book of Daniel that serves as today's first reading. It is there that we discover "one like a Son of man," a celestial being to whom "dominion, glory, and kingship" were given by God. But how could they ever have imagined, much less comprehend, that Jesus would bring to fulfillment all of the expectations attached to this mysterious Son of man?

Finally, what was the topic of the conversation that took place between Jesus, Moses, and Elijah? They were discussing Jesus' upcoming "exodus," his "going out." The word *exodus* immediately calls to mind ancient Israel's departure from Egyptian bondage. Most commentators maintain that this is a reference to Jesus' death outside of Jerusalem. If this is the case, one can argue that his death was not a tragic mistake, something that Jesus was unable to avoid. If he was discussing it with Moses and Elijah, then his death was known beforehand by the two men who represented the entire religious tradition of Israel. Perhaps he was explaining to them what he would later explain to the two disciples on the road to Emmaus: "Then beginning with Moses and all the prophets, he interpreted to them what referred to him in all the scriptures" (Luke 24:27).

In Luke's Gospel, Jesus prays before many important events occur. In the gospel for today, the text does not say that he went up the mountain to be transfigured, but to pray. It was while he was in prayer that he was transfigured. This episode is a kind of linchpin, linking a past event with a future one. The voice from the cloud and the words spoken are reminiscent of aspects of Jesus' baptism, the event that launched his public ministry. The brilliant change in Jesus' appearance looks forward to his transformation at the time of his resurrection. Since Peter, John, and James are the three apostles who would later witness Jesus' agony in the garden, it only seems right that they should have a foretaste of his glorification.

By some horrible coincidence, we recall the brilliance of Jesus' appearance on the very day that the world marks another cosmic event, the explosion of the first atomic bomb over Hiroshima. The paradox contained in the proximity of these two events should not be lost. The white light that shone from Christ was a mere suggestion of the divine splendor that is beyond human comprehension; the flashing light from the atomic explosion was an omen of the destructive force that is within human grasp. It is our responsibility during our lifetime to make sure that the horror of the latter event is brought under the control of the glory of the former one.

Praying with Scripture

- Pray for a strengthening of your faith so that you might be able to believe what appears to be unbelievable.

- How well do you know the relationship between the ancient Israelite expectations and the manner in which Jesus fulfilled them? If not well enough, what might you do to change this?

- On this anniversary of the Hiroshima tragedy, recommit yourself to a peaceful way of resolving your differences with others.

ASSUMPTION OF THE BLESSED VIRGIN MARY (SOLEMNITY)

Readings:
Rev 11:19a; 12:1–6a, 10ab; Ps 45:10–12, 16; 1 Cor 15:20–27; Luke 1:39–56

HAIL, HOLY QUEEN

What can we say about the assumption of Mary? There is no mention of it in the scriptures. That, of course, does not invalidate the feast. It simply means that its full theological meaning is found outside of the biblical tradition. The readings assigned for this feast do, however, provide us with insight into the early church's rich and varied tradition regarding the mother of Jesus.

The cosmic imagery in the first reading, which is from the Book of Revelation, is startling in its extravagance, dynamism, and reversal. We first see a woman "clothed with the sun, with the moon beneath her feet." She cries aloud in labor as her son is being born. Upon his birth, he is caught up into heaven with God, but the woman flees into the desert in order to escape the huge red dragon that seeks to devour her child. The imagery creates stunning theater, but it is not meant simply to entertain. Profound theology is expressed in these metaphors. This woman enjoys a place of prominence in heaven. Clearly her importance is found in her role as the mother of the child who was "destined to rule all the nations." The passage further describes a battle between a huge red dragon and the woman's newborn child. This scene calls to mind one depicted in the Genesis account of the first sin, where the offspring of the serpent is at war with the offspring of the first woman. Though the reading probably initially had no bearing on Mary's assumption into heaven, its selection for this feast underscores her maternal role on the cosmic stage of redemption.

The Letter to the Corinthians states that the Risen Christ is "the firstfruits of those who have fallen asleep," and that "in Christ shall all be brought to life, but each one in proper order." Since it was from Mary's flesh that the savior was born, it seems only right that she should be the first after her son to share in the power of his resurrection. The feast that we celebrate today marks the early church's belief that the human body that bore Jesus was preserved from the physical corruption that will be the lot of all other human beings.

In some circles, devotion to Mary has waned over the recent past. The image of a docile wife and a stay-at-home mother who is dependent upon others for support has lost its appeal. The image of Mary that is offered in today's gospel, however, paints an entirely different picture. Though she is with child, she sets aside her own comfort and journeys to the hill country to visit and care for an older relative who will soon give birth. In that culture, it would probably be quite unusual for a woman, particularly one in such a delicate condition, to travel by herself, and yet the text makes no mention of a traveling companion. This does not necessarily mean that she actually was alone—it does mean that such a possible companion was not important in the story.

Mary's visit to Elizabeth set the stage for the recognition of her unborn child by the child in Elizabeth's womb. After Mary and Joseph, Elizabeth was the first person to realize the identity of Mary's child: "How does this happen to me, that the mother of my

Lord should come to me?" Mary's prayer in response to this acknowledgment is reminiscent of the victory hymns of Miriam after the people had crossed the sea and escaped from Egypt (Exod 15:1–18), of Hannah when she offered her son Samuel to the service of God (1 Sam 2:1–10), and of Judith upon freeing the Israelites from the grip of the Assyrian general Holofernes (Jdt 16:1–17).

In her prayer, Mary first gives praise to God for granting her a dignity that will eventually be recognized by all. She then thanks God for having cared for the lowly and the poor, for having fed the hungry, and for having humbled the arrogant. This is a prayer of praise and thanksgiving and victory. While it is certainly profoundly religious, it is also noticeably political. Mary is concerned with issues of social justice and the future of the nation. She is a self-determined, politically astute, and socially sensitive individual, certainly the kind of person modern women could emulate. Ascribing a prayer such as this to Mary associates her with those noble women of the past, and the role that she plays in the drama of salvation compares with the roles that they played. Mary was instrumental in the deliverance of God's people from the bondage of sin, as Miriam was in the deliverance from Egyptian bondage. Like Hannah before her, at the presentation of her son in the Temple, she realized that he was destined for the total service of God. Now, as queen of heaven, she intercedes for her people as Judith did for hers. We may not understand the depth of the mystery of Mary's assumption, but we can certainly appreciate the role that she plays on our behalf as a queen of heaven who continues to be concerned for the welfare of her children.

Praying with Scripture

- What about Mary most inspires you? How might you imitate this characteristic?

- Make an effort this week to perform at least one act that might further justice in the world.

- Pray the Hail Mary slowly and thoughtfully, reflecting on each of the phrases.

EXALTATION OF THE HOLY CROSS (FEAST)

Readings:
Num 21:4b–9; Ps 78:1–2, 34–38;
Phil 2:6–11; John 3:13–17

WHAT DOESN'T KILL YOU MAKES YOU STRONGER!

"What doesn't kill you makes you stronger!" Recently, this expression has become a rather popular way of explaining how one has been able to draw good out of a difficult situation. It is also used to encourage those who are struggling. It is a much stronger statement than an earlier one: "When life gives you lemons, make lemonade." There is truth in both expressions. Suffering does require that we reach deep down into ourselves in order to discover there strengths we may not have known we possessed. There is no guarantee, of course, that we will come out of our trials a better person. We may simply be soured by the lemons thrust upon us by life, or the ordeal facing us just might kill us after all. Today's feast provides a startling twist to that first expression. All of the readings assigned to this day claim that what kills you can actually make you stronger. At least what killed Jesus made him stronger, and we are strengthened as we participate in that death.

The first reading might be considered a short play in four acts: (1) the people who have just been delivered from Egyptian bondage complain about the absence of food; (2) they are afflicted by fiery serpent bites for their lack of trust in God; (3) repenting of their infidelity, they plead with Moses to intercede for them; (4) directed by God, Moses sets up a kind of talisman through which God heals those who look upon it with faith. The story follows the pattern found in many of the stories in the Book of Judges: the people sin; God punishes them; they repent; God sends them a savior. Following this pattern one might say that, by the power of God, the bronze serpent acted as a savior. The twist in this story occurs when the animal that killed also healed.

This story must have been a familiar one to the Jewish people at the time of Jesus, for he employs it in his instruction to Nicodemus, as we read in the gospel passage. Jesus compares the lifting up of the serpent that had been mounted on a pole to his own being lifted up on the cross. Just as those in the wilderness who looked to the serpent with faith in God were healed of death from the serpent's bite, so those who looked to Jesus with faith in him are healed of whatever might deny them eternal life.

What follows in the gospel is one of the best-known biblical passages: "God so loved the world that he gave his only Son." It is this passage that revolutionizes the theory of retribution that lies behind the story from Numbers, a theory claiming that the good will be rewarded and the wicked will be punished. This theory is really the foundation of justice, and it should be revered as such. Justice is not the dominant dynamic operative when we are talking about God's disposition toward us, however; rather, it is love. And it is not love for those who are faithful, love for those who might seem to deserve it. It is a love for sinners, a love that cannot be explained. It is a love that would prompt God to send the divine Son to sacrifice his life for the sake of others. This is not an unyielding love for truth and justice; it is a tender love for weak human beings.

As a child, I did not find this image of God completely satisfying. True, I was happy in the fact that God loved me so much, but I always felt bad for Jesus. Why would God make him suffer like that when he didn't do anything wrong? I didn't know at the time that the second reading for this feast would have answered my question: that "he emptied himself." It was not against his will that his life was sacrificed for us. Jesus was a more than willing participant in our redemption.

In these few verses from the Letter to Philippians, Paul carefully and succinctly brings together several mysteries of our faith. Christ Jesus who was true God emptied himself of all divine privilege and became a human being in order to bring us back to God. His wholehearted commitment to this goal cost him his life. Through his death, however, he was able to accomplish what he set out to do, and so was reinstated in his rightful place of glory at the right hand of God.

How does the cross fit into this? Are we glorifying an instrument of torture? By no means! The cross was the instrument of Jesus' salvific death and, therefore, it is the means of our redemption. Just as the horrible gashes in Jesus' hands and feet are now glorified and worthy of our veneration, so the cross is now a symbol of Jesus' love for us. When we honor the cross, as we do today, or venerate it, as we do on Good Friday, we are really humbly acknowledging divine love and our total dependence on it.

Praying with Scripture

- Spend some time today reflecting on ways God's love is made known in your life.

- Do you possess any religious symbols that remind you of that love? If not, think about getting one.

- To what lengths are you willing to go for the sake of others?

ALL SAINTS (SOLEMNITY)
Readings:
Rev 7:2–4, 9–14; Ps 24:1–6;
1 John 3:1–3; Matt 5:1–12a

BLESSED ARE YOU!

Just what makes a saint? As little children we learned that in order to be a saint, we have to obey our parents. As we grew older, we discovered that there were more commandments to observe. As we got still older, we came to the conclusion that being a saint really wasn't going to be much fun. At that time we had to make a decision. Were we going to pursue the path of holiness, or would we go in another direction, still observing the commandments, but doing so in a way that was reasonable? We came to realize that assuming our place in the world was going to be challenging enough. We did not really need any extraordinary demonstrations of heroism. In making that decision, we joined the ranks of so many people who are content to be good, when they could really be better—even great.

Who are the saints that we honor today? What did they do that made them so great? The reading from Revelation tells us that they are "those who had been marked with the seal." Probably a mark made by some kind of signet ring, the seal was used on official documents or personal possessions. These people are sealed in order to set them apart from others. But whose seal? And why were they sealed? The reading also describes them as those who "have washed their robes and made them white in the blood of the Lamb." Since laundering clothes in blood will not make them white, we know that this reading is filled with symbolism.

The scene is of a future gathering of believers who survive the final eschatological distress. It is not a select group of martyrs who willingly *gave* their lives for the faith. It is "a great multitude, which no one could count, from every nation, race, people, and tongue," who willingly *lived* their lives for the faith. They were sealed by the sacraments of baptism and confirmation, and they were redeemed by "the blood of the Lamb." This is a picture of members of the glorified church who, when their lives on earth are completed, stand before the throne of God and before the Lamb and cry out in praise. But what did they do on earth that gained them such an exalted place in heaven?

The reading from the First Letter of John clearly identifies the saints as those who are "the children of God." The author is not merely speaking about those who have died; he is speaking about all of us: "We are God's children." There is tenderness in this exclamation. The author seems to be saying that God's love is not yet finished with us. If God's love can make us children of God now, imagine what we will become when that love has totally transformed us! Did he have in mind the vast assembly of those who "have washed their robes and made them white in the blood of the Lamb"? The reading places responsibility on our shoulders. It states: "Everyone who has this hope based on [God] makes himself pure, as [God] is pure." In other words, we have to change.

The first reading speaks of washing one's robes in the blood of the Lamb; the second one says that we make ourselves pure; the gospel is much more specific about how this will be accomplished. There we find the list of wisdom adages known as the Beatitudes. They are pithy sayings describing the dynamics of the reign of God. Even a cursory glance shows that they are radical, counter-cultural directives. The poor in spirit are those who do not lust after the material benefits of this world; the meek are those who do not seek power over others. Those who mourn or who hunger for justice realize that as precious as life in this world might be, it cannot completely satisfy us. The merciful and the clean of heart are those who are motivated by religious piety. The peacemakers are those who work for reconciliation in the world. People whose lives reflect these attitudes are the children of God. And because pride and selfishness, hatred and violence so often gain control of so many human minds and hearts, these saints of God are frequently "persecuted for the sake of righteousness."

We all know about saints like these: the poor Francis, the meek Thérèse, the mournful Benedict Joseph Labre, justice's advocate Oscar Romero, the merciful John XXIII, the clean of heart Kateri Tekakwitha. And there are other saints: neighbors whose homes are always open to those in need; people whose humble service we take for granted, because we pay for it; families who mourn murdered love ones; those who place their personal freedom in jeopardy by protesting social injustice; parents who constantly show mercy to wayward children. And we all know good and decent women and men who are clean of heart. There is no reason why we cannot name ourselves among them.

Praying with Scripture

- How seriously do you take your baptismal commitment? Has it made a difference in the way you live your life?

- Whom do you consider is a saint? What characteristics does that person possess that makes you think this?

- Choose one of the Beatitudes, and this week perform at least one act that would flow from it.

ALL THE FAITHFUL DEPARTED (COMMEMORATION)
Readings:
Wis 3:1–9; Ps 23:1–6;
Rom 5:5–11; John 11:17–27

WHAT EVER HAPPENED TO PURGATORY?

In *The Divine Comedy*, Dante weaves a spellbinding account of his journey from hell, through purgatory, into heaven. With the Latin poet Virgil as his guide, he records the fate of the dead. Considered one of the greatest epic poems of all time, this medieval allegory continues to influence the popular perceptions of heaven, hell, and purgatory even to our day. While we still talk about heaven and hell, the idea of purgatory seems to have lost its importance, except at funerals when we pray: "Eternal rest grant unto them, O Lord, and let perpetual light shine upon them. May they rest in peace. Amen."

Why do we need purgatory? And why do we think our prayers and good works can lessen the duration of purgation of our beloved dead? Most people probably think that we need purgatory because we are imperfect human beings—which, of course, we are. The real focus here is not on human limitation, however, but on the holiness of God. Since only what is perfect is fit to appear before God, and since human weakness renders us all unworthy of that privilege, some form of purification was deemed necessary.

The idea of praying for the dead can be found in ancient Israel. When forbidden amulets were discovered on the bodies of slain Jewish soldiers, Judas Maccabees and his men "prayed that the sinful deed might be fully blotted out" (2 Macc 12:42). He then collected money "which he sent to Jerusalem to provide for an expiatory sacrifice" (12:43). Offering sacrifice for the reparation of sin was quite common in ancient Israel, but doing so for the dead was something new. Jewish converts to Christianity may simply have continued this practice. The church developed the practice of granting indulgences, a kind of waiver that granted remission of the punishment for sin. Believers were able to apply this remission to their own punishment as well as to the punishment of others. Though this practice became a bone of contention among various Christian churches, it continued to be quite popular until the Second Vatican Council. Since then, there is almost no talk about indulgences. One has to wonder: "Whatever happened to purgatory?"

The readings assigned for this commemoration provide insight into this question. The passage from Wisdom assures those grieving the death of the righteous that those good people are not lost. In fact, they are at peace in the tender hands of a loving God. Though there is mention of minimal chastisement and trial, the primary focus of the reading is on the goodness of God: "Grace and mercy are with his holy ones, and his care is with his elect."

The responsorial psalm characterizes God as a solicitous shepherd, one who cares for all the needs of the flock. The picture painted is one of carefree existence, peaceful rest, and abundant fruitfulness. The shepherd's protection is guaranteed by the presence of his rod and staff that were used to ward off wild animals as well as poachers. The valley of "deep darkness" has meaning on several levels. While it may originally have referred to the actual terrain of the place of shepherding, it can also be a metaphor for the gloom that can overwhelm an individual. This particular commemoration suggested a different interpretation, however, namely, death. Even in the face of this great terror, the psalmist claims to be unafraid, for the presence of the LORD is reassuring. Here too, the focus is on the goodness of God.

Divine love is also discussed in the passage from the Letter to the Romans. One point pertinent to the matter under consideration here is the fact that "while we were still sinners Christ died for us." Furthermore, "if, while we were enemies, we were reconciled to God through the death of his Son, how much more, once reconciled, will we be saved by his life"? As with the first reading and the responsorial psalm, this reading acknowledges human sinfulness, but it too argues that such sinfulness is eclipsed by the bounteous love of God.

Finally, the gospel passage depicts Jesus comforting Martha at the death of her brother. After assuring her that Lazarus will rise again, she professes her faith in the resurrection of the dead, a faith held by many Pharisaic Jews of the time. But Jesus then makes a startling claim: "I am the resurrection and the life; he who believes in me, even if he dies, will live." The call here is for faith in Jesus and trust in divine solicitude. Jesus does not explain how this will happen. He simply asks her if she believes that it will.

With this focus on divine solicitude, whatever happened to purgatory? Without denying our sinfulness, we have come to view the trials and tribulations of life as opportunities for the necessary purification we all need. And what about praying for the dead? Such prayers keep us connected with those who have gone before us, those "souls of the just [that] are in the hand of God."

Praying with Scripture

- Spend some time thinking of your deceased family members and friends. Then commit them to the loving care of God.

- Reflect on your own death, and pray for the grace to trust in God's love for you.

- Develop the habit of comforting the grieving whenever you have the opportunity of doing so.

DEDICATION OF THE LATERAN BASILICA (FEAST)
Readings:
Ezek 47:1–2, 8–9, 12; Ps 46:2–3, 5–6, 8–9; 1 Cor 3:9c–11, 16–17; John 2:13–22

IT'S JUST A BUILDING!

Not long ago, the parish of my childhood was closed. It was not merged; it was closed. Years ago, a new church structure replaced the building in which my sister and I were baptized and she was married. I remember that old church fondly; the squeaky stairs leading up to the choir loft; the large room in the basement where I ate many breakfasts and dinners and danced at wedding receptions. My family left that parish before the old church had been taken down, but it will always be the church of my childhood. Some might say: "It was just a building!" But I disagree. It was the house of God, the place where I met God in a very special way.

The church building tells us a lot about how we understand the church community. Old churches, even small ones, were built with graceful arches, lofty ceilings, and towering steeples. This upward direction was meant to lift our minds and hearts to heaven. The pews were arranged so that all eyes could be riveted on the sacred mysteries that were enacted on the altar, which sat against the front wall. We watched; the action was too sacred for us to join. Silence was observed, because churches were considered places of prayer. They were certainly more than just buildings.

Today's churches reflect a very different theology. Everything about them bespeaks community participation. The very name, church, comes from the Greek word *ekklesía*, which means "assembly," not "building." To the extent that it is possible, the altar, which is now referred to as the eucharistic table, is situated in the center with the pews arranged around it. Ceilings have been lowered for purposes of acoustics, and attention is sometimes directed to walls on which the words of hymns might be projected. These churches are places of community gathering and sharing, and so silence is replaced by the warm greetings of friends.

Neither in the past nor today is the church just a building. It is the place where religious activity unfolds. It is the place where, in a very special way, we join with our sisters and brothers in faith and together we pray to and encounter God. True, all of this can take place anywhere, in any building, even in the open air. But a church is specially dedicated for just such a purpose, and for no other. In traditional societies, temples were often constructed on the *axis mundi*, the "axis of the world." People believed that this was the spot where heaven, the earth, and the underworld came together, and for this reason it was considered sacred. Temples were also built on high mountains, since such elevations were believed to be the closest place to the heavens. It should be clear from this that they too were seen as more than just buildings.

Today we commemorate the dedication of the Lateran Basilica. It is the cathedral church of Rome, the official church of the pope, and, consequently, it is considered the "Mother Church" of all churches. The readings remind us just how important a church building can be. The first passage contains a report of one of Ezekiel's visionary experiences. In it the prophet is brought to the door of the Temple and from there he is able to observe a stream of water flowing from the threshold of the Temple. The stream grows in force until it becomes a mighty river, and the river waters the entire land, enabling it to produce fruits in abundance. Though the river is depicted as the source of life of every living creature, the real source of life is the Temple. The image of a river that is the source of life is also found in the responsorial psalm. There its runlets gladden the city of God, the place where God dwells. It is clear that here too, the holy dwelling of the Most High, the Temple, is more than just a building.

During Jesus' lifetime, the Temple was the center of the religious life of the Jewish nation. It was there that the prescribed sacrifices were offered to God, and it was to the Temple that observant Jews traveled to celebrate the three pilgrimage festivals of Passover, Pentecost, and Tabernacles. Because Jews came from all over the world to worship there, and because only official Temple coins were acceptable as an offering, certain commercial transactions were deemed necessary. This is the background for Jesus' angry words: "Take these out of here, and stop making my Father's house a marketplace." It is clear from his words that he considered the Temple the dwelling place of God. It is also clear that he believed its sacred character was being undermined.

Today's readings help us to appreciate the importance of any building that is considered the dwelling place of God on earth. Most of us will probably never have the opportunity of visiting the Lateran Basilica in Rome, but today we join with all the people of God in all the churches of the world to celebrate the dedication of our "Mother Church."

Praying with Scripture

- Spend some time before the liturgy today reflecting on the importance of your parish church as the special dwelling place of God.

- What do you do to build up your local parish community? What more might you do?

- Pray for the grace to realize that, though we participate in the church on the local level, we are really members of a worldwide community, with connections to people everywhere.

IMMACULATE CONCEPTION (SOLEMNITY)
Readings:
Gen 3:9–15, 20; Ps 98:1–4;
Eph 1:3–6, 11–12; Luke 1:26–38

CHOSEN TO BE HOLY

The readings for the feast of the Immaculate Conception are rich in meaning, but they are frequently misunderstood when viewed through the lens of the feast itself. This is true for at least two major reasons. First, contrary to some artistic depictions of Mary as the Immaculate Conception, the Genesis account that lies behind this image states that it is the woman's offspring who will strike the serpent's head, rather than the woman, as statues and pictures depict. Furthermore, the gospel reading for the solemnity recounts the annunciation and miraculous conception of Jesus, not the Immaculate Conception of Mary. It is no wonder there is confusion in the minds of many people. Nonetheless, the solemnity really does hold significance for us.

All of the readings for today speak of God's tender mercy and saving action on behalf of sinners. Despite the constant hostility that God warns will exist between the serpent and the woman, between the various manifestations of temptation and her children (Gen 3:15), God has given sinful people chance after chance to start again. This can be seen not only in the reading itself, but also in all the annals of human history. Though people are often punished for their sins, such punishment is no indication of divine abandonment. It may be seen as a corrective. What is important is that God gives us another chance. This is precisely what we find in this reading. The offspring of the woman will himself take on the conflict with the offspring of the tempter. Throughout their lives, human beings may have to battle temptation, but the passage suggests that they will not be vanquished.

The responsorial psalm characterizes God as a strong warrior: "His right hand has won victory for him." The psalmist may have originally been thinking of a victory that transpired on the stage of Israel's political experience, but an even earlier image of God the victorious warrior is cosmic in character. It refers to the primordial conquest of the forces of good over the forces of evil. This is the victory of which the reading from Genesis speaks. Since the psalm verses are a response to this reading, one can say that this is the victory intended here. Thus, though human beings will be in constant conflict with temptation and the forces of evil, God will be on their side and this great warrior God is always victorious.

Paul too directs our attention to "the foundation of the world" as he insists, in the Letter to the Ephesians, that we were chosen by God from the very beginning of time. He is not here speaking of predestination as it has come to be understood in some Christian traditions, a predestination in which some are preordained for salvation while others are preordained for damnation. According to Paul, all are destined for salvation. He further explains that we were not chosen because we *are* holy and blameless, but for the opposite reason. We were chosen so that we *might become* holy and blameless. Salvation is the cause of our holiness; it is not its reward. Furthermore, Christ is the one through whom all of this is accomplished.

Though the gospel account concentrates on the angels' announcement to Mary, the passage is really the prelude to the story of God's saving action through Christ, the offspring who will ultimately crush the head of evil. Gabriel addresses Mary as "full of grace." What did "full of grace" mean? Today we know that it means that Mary had been preserved from the sin that afflicts all of us. In her response, Mary does not question *that* all of this will happen according to God's plan, but she wonders *how* it will happen. There is in her a willingness to accept God's plan that was absent from the woman in the Genesis account. The plan of God has now come full circle. A woman played a significant role in the commission of sin, and a woman plays a similar role in the drama of salvation. What Paul says is true of us is also true of Mary. She was not chosen to be the mother of the Messiah because she was holy and blameless. Rather, she was made holy and blameless because she was to be the mother of the Messiah.

We may not be able to claim such extraordinary privileges for ourselves, but we too have been chosen, called by God to participate in God's work of salvation; we too exist for the praise of God's glory. We must never forget that the extraordinary nature of Mary's privilege did not exempt her from ordinary, perhaps even humdrum, life. She did not stand apart because of the kind of life she lived, but rather because of the quality of her living that life. In this, she can be a model for all of us, chosen by God and set apart to be holy while living faithfully within the particular circumstances of life.

Praying with Scripture

- Reflect on some times when God gave you another chance, and give thanks.

- What are some of the spiritual blessings with which God has favored you? In what ways do you think they have kept you from sinning?

- Pray the Hail Mary slowly and thoughtfully, taking time to reflect on Mary's special blessings.